GO!®

CUT TIME. QUILT MORE.™

FALL/WINTER 2018 CATALOG

NEW

GO! me™
EASY FABRIC PROJECT MAKER

creative fabric projects

fun

inspiring projects to spark the imagination

Includes:
GO! Me™ Fabric Cutter
2 GO!® Dies
Cutting Mat

ⓐ accuquilt®

THE ACCUQUILT GO!® CUTTER FAMILY

Developed for ease of use, easy storage and saving time, AccuQuilt® products include a premier line of fabric cutting systems. GO!® fabric cutters cut up to six layers of 100% cotton at a time. Plus, over 200 GO! fabric cutting dies have been created for use with the different fabric cutters. More than 1000 quilting patterns and a wide range of quilting resources are also available to help quilters.

Along with our ever expanding line of dies, AccuQuilt recently introduced the GO! Me™ Easy Fabric Project Maker. GO! Me introduces the next generation to the art of sewing & quilting with projects that advance with their skill level.

Fall in Love with Quilting All Over Again.®

Media Code DC1810G. Prices effective November 1, 2018. All prices are in USD. AccuQuilt retains the right to change pricing and discontinue items at any time, without prior notice. ©201
AccuQuilt. Designs ©1990-2018 AccuQuilt. Any reproductions of these designs, in a form other than cutouts made from steel-rule dies manufactured exclusively by AccuQuilt, is a violation
of federal copyright law. AccuQuilt will prosecute any copyright cinfringements to the fullest extent of the law.

GO! CUTTER COLLECTION:
Everyone has a dream fabric cutter. Let's find yours! Our state-of-the-art machines are accurate, effortless and 90% faster than rotary cutters.

GO! ME™ EASY FABRIC PROJECT MAKER:
Includes everything kids and tweens, need to have wildly inventive fun creating fabric projects.

GO! QUBE™ DIE SETS:
Sew by numbers! Cut perfect blocks with our easy numbering system.

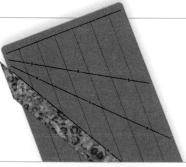

STRIP CUTTERS WITH ANGLED GUIDE LINES:
Silkscreened guidelines make it easy to align fabric and subcut shapes to the sizes you need.

BLOCK ON BOARD® (BOB®):
Create a complete block with all the shapes on one die board.

TWO TONE™ FOAM:
Makes it quick and easy to align fabric over blades so you can save fabric.

DOG-EARED CORNERS & ¼" SEAM ALLOWANCE:
More time quilting and no time clipping!

NOTCHES:
Line up the notches for accurate cuts and easy piecing of curvy quilt designs.

FIND OUT WHY ACCUQUILT GO!® IS A CUT ABOVE THE REST

CONTENTS

It's the perfect gift

for nieces, nephews, children, and grandchildren on your holiday gift giving list.

GO!
me

All prices are USD.

Register your GO!® product on accuquilt.com

GO!me™

EASY FABRIC PROJECT MAKER

IMAGINE. CUT. CREATE.

AccuQuilt is excited to introduce you to the new GO! Me™ Easy Fabric Project Maker. It includes everything kids and tweens need to have wildly inventive fun creating great projects from start to finish.

INCLUDES:
- GO! Me™ Fabric Cutter
- 2 GO! Dies:
  - Owl (existing) + Owl Accessories (New)
  - Pattern insert included with each die
- Fabric (felt) and thread included to make first project (Owl Animal Buddy)
- 6"x6" Cutting Mat
- Pattern booklet
- User's Manual

- Works with over 130 GO!® Dies!
- Cutter Weight: 8.5 lbs. (3.9 kg)
- Boxed Weight: 10.5 lbs. (4.8 kg)
- Closed: 12½"W x 4½"L x 8¼"H (includes handle)
- Open: 17"W x 12½"L x 8¼"H (includes handle)

$199.99 (55275)

READY. SET. GO!®

ULTIMATE FABRIC CUTTING SYSTEM

The Ready. Set. GO!® Ultimate Fabric Cutting System includes everything you need to get started in one box. You get the GO! Fabric Cutter, 8" GO! Qube Mix & Match Block, GO! Qube Book by Eleanor Burns, GO! Strip Cutter – 2½" Die, GO! Qube DVD & die pick, 2 cutting mats, pattern and idea book.

- Box Weight: 38 lbs (17.2 kg)

$449.99* (55700)

SAVE OVER $220*

GREAT BUNDLE PRICE!

*Compare to $672.89, $222.90 savings when all products are purchased separately.

GO!®
FABRIC CUTTER
STARTER SET

The GO!® Fabric Cutter is perfect for everyday quilters, students and hobbyists. Like all of our cutters, you'll be able to cut up to six layers of fabric quickly and easily. With its portable design, you can take it with you wherever you want to quilt.

- Cutter Weight: 15 lbs. (6.8 kg)
- Boxed Weight: 20 lbs (9.1 kg)
- Closed: 17"W x 5"L x 15"H (includes handle)
- Open: 30½"W x 17"L x 6¼"H (includes handle)

$299.99 (55100S)

SET INCLUDES:
GO! Fabric Cutter, GO! Value die with 3 shapes, cutting mat, die pick and pattern book

GO! BIG®
ELECTRIC FABRIC CUTTER
STARTER SET

The GO! Big® Electric Fabric Cutter is our fastest and largest cutter. You can use up to two dies at a time, and up to six layers of fabric. Plus, its fully-automatic design means it's perfect for everyone, especially arthritis sufferers. Compatible with all GO! and GO! Big Dies.

- Cutter Weight: 23 lbs. (10.4 kg)
- Boxed Weight: 28 lbs. (12.7 kg)
- Closed: 19"W x 6"L x 11"H
- Open: 19"W x 18"L x 6"H

$599.99 (55500)

SET INCLUDES:
GO! Big Electric Fabric Cutter, GO! Flying Geese die, cutting mat and pattern book.

One button. Fully automatic for ease of use with built-in safety features.

GO! Value Die not included.

INSPIRATION & ORGANIZATION - IN ONE BOXED SET.

The GO! Qube Mix & Match Blocks take cutting fabric pieces to a whole new dimension. You'll love the versatility and endless design options this system provides. The convenient die numbering system gives you the ability to combine shapes in different ways to create 72 block patterns with ease. Add GO! Qube Companion Set – Corners (page 10) and GO! Qube Companion Set – Angles (page 12) to expand your block options to 216 and beyond!

THE GO! QUBE™ MIX & MATCH SET INCLUDES:

- 8 Mix & Match GO! Dies
- Cutting mat & storage box
- Instructional DVD & pattern book
- 14 FREE patterns
- Available in 6", 8", 9", 10" and 12" finished block sizes

GO! Qube™ Mix & Match 6" Block
Makes 6" finished blocks. 55775****
$219.99
Compare to $264.90* • $44.91 savings!

GO! Qube™ Mix & Match 8" Block
Makes 8" finished blocks. 55776****
$219.99
Compare to $264.90* • $44.91 savings!

GO! Qube™ Mix & Match 9" Block
Makes 9" finished blocks. 55777****
$219.99
Compare to $264.90* • $44.91 savings!

NEW

GO! Qube™ Mix & Match 10" Block
Makes 10" finished blocks. 55797**
$279.99
Compare to $352.89* $72.90 savings!

GO! Qube™ Mix & Match 12" Block
Makes 12" finished blocks. 55778**
$279.99
Compare to $352.89* $72.90 savings!

Compatible with GO! Big® ✱ GO!® ✱ GO! Baby® ✱ GO! Me™ ✱ *If all dies and mats were purchased separately.

GO! Qube-6" (55775), 8" (55776), 9" (55777): 6.5 lbs. (3 kg), 6⅞"W x 7⅜"L x 6¾"H • GO! Qube-10" (55797) & GO! Qube-12" (55778): 13.4 lbs. (6 kg), 10⅞"W x 7⅜"L x 10⅞"H

Use this chart to find which numbers on the blocks coordinate with GO! Qubes & dies listed.

GO! Qube™ Item #'s (listed first) or GO! Die Item #'s (sold separately)

Shape Number	6" Finished Block	8" Finished Block	9" Finished Block	10" Finished Block	12" Finished Block
1	GO! Square - 3½" (3" Finished) 55775 or 55006	GO! Square - 4½" (4" Finished) 55776, 55060 or 55018	GO! Square - 5" (4½" Finished) 55777 or 55010	GO! Square - 5½" (5" Finished) 55797*	GO! Square - 6½" (6" Finished) 55778* or 55000*
2	GO! Square - 2" (1½" Finished) 55775 or 55022	GO! Square - 2½" (2" Finished) 55776, 55059 or 55018	GO! Square - 2¾" (2¼" Finished) 55777 or 55395	GO! Square - 3" (2½" Finished) 55797 or 55256	GO! Square - 3½" (3" Finished) 55778 or 55006
3	GO! Half Square Triangle - 3" Finished Square 55775 or 55009	GO! Half Square Triangle - 4" Finished Square 55776 or 55031	GO! Half Square Triangle 4½" Finished Square 55777 or 55397	GO! Half Square Triangle 5" Finished Square 55797*	GO! Half Square Triangle 6" Finished Square 55778* or 55001*
4	GO! Quarter Square Triangle - 3" Finished Square 55775 or 55396	GO! Quarter Square Triangle - 4" Finished Square 55776, 55316 or 55047	GO! Quarter Square Triangle - 4½" Finished Square 55777 or 55398	GO! Quarter Square Triangle - 5" Finished Square 55797*	GO! Quarter Square Triangle 6" Finished Square 55778*, 55002 or 55456
5	GO! Half Square Triangle - 1½" Finished Square 55775 or 55319	GO! Half Square Triangle - 2" Finished Square 55776, 55063 or 55018	GO! Half Square Triangle - 2¼" Finished Square 55777 or 55147	GO! Half Square Triangle - 2½" Finished Square 55797 or 55257	GO! Half Square Triangle 3" Finished Square 55778, 55009 or 55456
6	GO! Square on Point - 2⅝" (2⅛" Finished) 55775 or 55394	GO! Square on Point - 3¼" (2¾" Finished) 55776 or 55317	GO! Square on Point - 3¹¹⁄₁₆" (3³⁄₁₆" Finished) 55777 or 55106	GO! Square on Point - 3¹⁄₁₆" (3⁹⁄₁₆" Finished) 55797*	GO! Square on Point - 4¾" (4¼" Finished) 55778 or 55019
7	GO! Parallelogram 45°- 2¼" x 2¹³⁄₁₆" Sides (1½" x 2⅛" Finished) 55775 or 55402	GO! Parallelogram 45°- 2¾" x 3½" Sides (2¹⁄₁₆" x 2¹³⁄₁₆" Finished) 55776 or 55318	GO! Parallelogram 45°- 2¹⁵⁄₁₆" x 3⅞" Sides (2¼" x 3³⁄₁₆" Finished) 55777 or 55148	GO! Parallelogram 45°- 3³⁄₁₆" x 4¼" Sides (2½" x 3⁹⁄₁₆" Finished) 55797*	GO! Parallelogram 45°- 3¹¹⁄₁₆" x 4¹⁵⁄₁₆" Sides (3" x 4¼" Finished) 55778* or 55004
8	GO! Rectangle - 2" x 3½" (1½" x 3" Finished) 55775 or 55158	GO! Rectangle - 2½" x 4½" (2" x 4" Finished) 55776 or 55159	GO! Rectangle - 2¾" x 5" (2¼" x 4½" Finished) 55777 or 55107	GO! Rectangle - 3" x 5½" (2½" x 5" Finished) 55797*	GO! Rectangle - 3½" x 6½" (3" x 6" Finished) 55778* or 55005

*Not compatible with GO! Baby® or GO! Me™

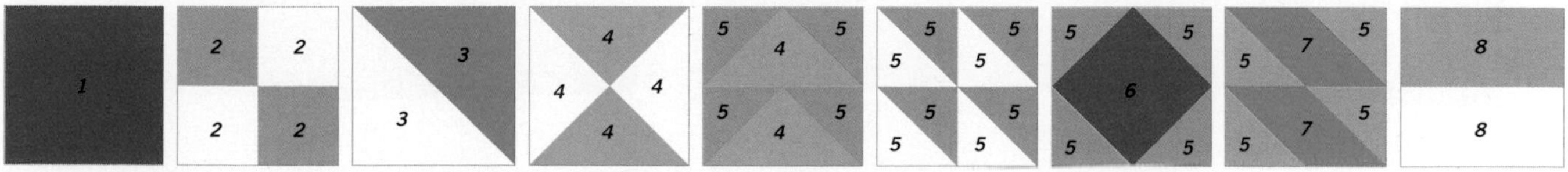

THIS SET IS ALL ABOUT THE CORNERS.

The NEW GO! Qube Companion Set – Corners expands the number of quilt blocks that the GO! Mix & Match Blocks can make from 72 to over 144 blocks. That number increases to 216 when added to the GO! Qube Companion Set – Angles! The boxed sets come in the sizes of 6", 8", 9", 10" and 12" and are designed to be the perfect companion to the existing GO! Qube sets of the same corresponding size.

GO! Qube™ Companion Sets – Corners are designed to work with GO! Qube Mix & Match Blocks...just add fabric!™

THE GO! QUBE™ COMPANION SET - CORNERS:

- Four GO! dies that work with existing GO! Qube Mix and Match Sets: Chisels, Signature Block, Bowtie, Half Square Triangle
- Cutting mat & storage box
- Instructional DVD & pattern book
- 10 FREE patterns
- Available in 6", 8", 9", 10" and 12" finished block sizes

GO! Qube™ 8" Twirling Petals Quilt

Expand the possibilities.

GO! Qube™ 6" Companion Set – Corners
Use with GO! Qube 6" Block (55775)
to make 6" finished blocks. 55784****
$129.99
Compare to $149.94* • $19.95 savings!

GO! Qube™ 8" Companion Set – Corners
Use with GO! Qube 8" Block (55776)
to make 8" finished blocks. 55785****
$129.99
Compare to $149.94* • $19.95 savings!

GO! Qube™ 9" Companion Set – Corners
Use with GO! Qube 9" Block (55777)
to make 9" finished blocks. 55786****
$129.99
Compare to $149.94* • $19.95 savings!

GO! Qube™ 10" Companion Set – Corners
Use with GO! Qube 10" Block (55797)
to make 10" finished blocks. 55798**
$169.99
Compare to $207.94*
$37.95 savings!

GO! Qube™ 12" Companion Set – Corners
Use with GO! Qube 12" Block (55778)
to make 12" finished blocks. 55787**
$169.99
Compare to $207.94*
$37.95 savings!

Compatible with GO! Big® ✱ GO!® ✱ GO! Baby® ✱ GO! Me™ ✱ *If all dies and mats were purchased separately.

NOTE: YOU MUST OWN A GO! QUBE™ MIX & MATCH SET BEFORE ADDING THE SAME-SIZED COMPANION SET.

Shape Number	6" Finished Block	8" Finished Block	9" Finished Block	10" Finished Block	12" Finished Block
9	GO! Chisels – 1½" x 3" Finished 55784	GO! Chisels – 2" x 4" Finished 55785	GO! Chisels – 2¼" x 4½" Finished 55786	GO! Chisels – 2½" x 5" Finished 55798*	GO! Chisels – 3" x 6" Finished 55787* or 55039
10	GO! Signature Block – 3" Finished Square 55784	GO! Signature Block – 4" Finished Square 55785	GO! Signature Block – 4½" Finished Square 55786	GO! Signature Block – 5" Finished Square 55798*	GO! Signature Block – 6" Finished Square 55787*
11.1	GO! Bowtie – 3" Finished Square 55784 or 55793	GO! Bowtie – 4" Finished Square 55785 or 55794	GO! Bowtie – 4½" Finished Square 55786 or 55795	GO! Bowtie – 5" Finished Square 55798*	GO! Bowtie – 6" Finished Square 55787* or 55796*
12.1	GO! Half Square Triangle – ¾" Finished Square 55784 or 55793	GO! Half Square Triangle – 1" Finished Square 55785 or 55794	GO! Half Square Triangle – 1⅛" Finished Square 55786 or 55795	GO! Half Square Triangle – 1¼" Finished Square 55798*	GO! Half Square Triangle – 1½" Finished Square 55787* or 55796*

*Not compatible with GO! Baby® or GO! Me™

FIND YOUR ANGLE.

The GO! Qube Companion Set – Angles expands the number of quilt blocks that the GO! Mix & Match Blocks can make from 72 to over 144 blocks. That number increases to 216 when added to the GO! Qube Companion Set – Corners! The boxed sets come in the sizes of 6", 8", 9", 10" and 12" and are designed to be the perfect companion to the existing GO! Qube sets of the same corresponding size.

GO! Qube™ Companion Sets – Angles are designed to work with GO! Qube Mix & Match Blocks…just add fabric!™

THE GO! QUBE™ COMPANION SET - ANGLES INCLUDES:

- Four GO! dies that work with existing GO! Qube Mix & Match Sets: Triangles in Square-Center, Triangles in Square-Sides, Kite and Trapezoid
- Cutting mat & storage box
- Instructional DVD & pattern book
- 10 FREE patterns
- Available in 6", 8", 9", 10" and 12" finished block sizes

GO! Qube™ 8" Patch Party Sampler Quilt

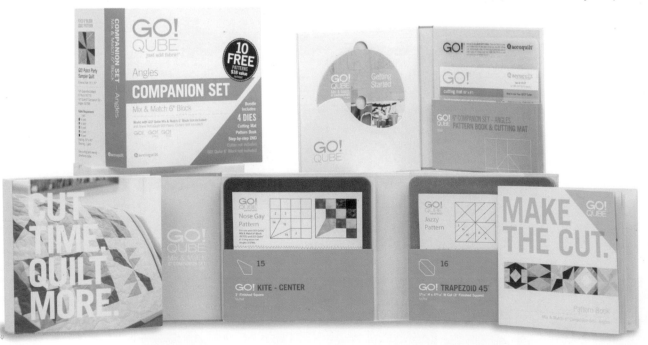

GO! Qube-6" (55788), 8" (55789), 9" (55790): 3.9 lbs. (1.8 kg), 6⁷⁄₈"W x 4¹⁄₈"L x 6³⁄₄"H • GO! Qube-10" (55799) & GO! Qube-12" (55791): 8.9 lbs. (4 kg), 10⁷⁄₈"W x 4¹⁄₈"L x 10⁷⁄₈"H

A smoother path to sharper angles.

GO! Qube™ 6" Companion Set — Angles
Use with GO! Qube 6" Block (55775)
to make 6" finished blocks. 55788****
$129.99
Compare to $149.94* • $19.95 savings!

GO! Qube™ 8" Companion Set — Angles
Use with GO! Qube 8" Block (55776)
to make 8" finished blocks. 55789****
$129.99
Compare to $149.94* • $19.95 savings!

GO! Qube™ 9" Companion Set — Angles
Use with GO! Qube 9" Block (55777)
to make 9" finished blocks. 55790****
$129.99
Compare to $149.94* • $19.95 savings!

GO! Qube™ 10" Companion Set — Angles
Use with GO! Qube 10" Block (55797)
to make 10" finished blocks. 55799**
$169.99
Compare to $207.94*
$37.95 savings!

GO! Qube™ 12" Companion Set — Angles
Use with GO! Qube 12" Block (55778)
to make 12" finished blocks. 55791**
$169.99
Compare to $207.94*
$37.95 savings!

Compatible with GO! Big® ✱ GO!® ✱ GO! Baby® ✱ GO! Me™ ✱ *If all dies and mats were purchased separately.

NOTE: YOU MUST OWN A GO! QUBE™ MIX & MATCH SET BEFORE ADDING THE SAME-SIZED COMPANION SET.

Shape Number	6" Finished Block	8" Finished Block	9" Finished Block	10" Finished Block	12" Finished Block
13	GO! Triangles in Square-Center — 3" Finished Square 55788 or 55027	GO! Triangles in Square-Center — 4" Finished Square 55789 or 55409	GO! Triangles in Square-Center — 4½" Finished Square 55790	GO! Triangles in Square-Center — 5" Finished Square 55799*	GO! Triangles in Square-Center — 6" Finished Square 55791*
14	GO! Triangles in Square-Sides — 3" Finished Square 55788 or 55027	GO! Triangles in Square-Sides — 4" Finished Square 55789 or 55409	GO! Triangles in Square-Sides — 4½" Finished Square 55790	GO! Triangles in Square-Sides — 5" Finished Square 55799*	GO! Triangles in Square-Sides — 6" Finished Square 55791*
15	GO! Kite-Center — 3" Finished Square 55788	GO! Kite-Center — 4" Finished Square 55789 or 55254	GO! Kite-Center — 4½" Finished Square 55790	GO! Kite-Center — 5" Finished Square 55799*	GO! Kite-Center — 6" Finished Square 55791*
16	GO! Trapezoid 45° — 1³⁄₁₆"H x 4¹⁵⁄₁₆"W Cut (3" Finished Square) 55788	GO! Trapezoid 45° — 1¹⁵⁄₁₆"H x 6⅜"W Cut (4" Finished Square) 55789	GO! Trapezoid 45° — 2¹⁄₁₆"H x 7¹⁄₁₆"W Cut (4½" Finished Square) 55790	GO! Trapezoid 45° — 2¼"H x 7¼"W Cut (5" Finished Square) 55799*	GO! Trapezoid 45° — 2⅝"H x 9³⁄₁₆"W Cut (6" Finished Square) 55791*

*Not compatible with GO! Baby® or GO! Me™

A QUILTING CLASS IN A BOX.

The GO! Qube™ Specialty Set – Serendipity by Edyta Sitar will help you cut time and quilt more! Your creativity will know no bounds. The GO! Qube Serendipity Set produces beautiful piecing, appliqué and embroidery. Edyta will guide you every step of the way with instructional patterns, videos and even a block of the month.

GO! Qube™ Shooting Star Block by Edyta Sitar

THE GO! QUBE™ SPECIALTY SET – SERENDIPITY INCLUDES:

- 8 geometric & appliqué dies
- Cutting mat & storage box
- 9 FREE patterns
- 21 Embroidery designs on CD
- Instructional DVD
- Works with all GO!® Cutters

Designer Edyta Sitar

GO! Qube™ Blooming Block of the Month Quilt by Edyta Sitar

GO! Qube™ Specialty Set – Serendipity by Edyta Sitar
Makes 5" and 10" finished blocks.
55783****

$279.99

Compare to $309.90*
$29.91 savings!

Works with all GO!® Cutters.

GO! Qube Specialty Set-Serendipity (55783): 6.5 lbs. (3 kg), 6⅞"W x 7⅜"L x 6¾"H

GO! Strip Cutter dies are a must when cutting a lot of strips. Die blades are 23" long and open at both ends; designed to cut folded fabric right off the bolt – up to 6 layers at a time!

STRIP CUTTERS WITH ANGLED GUIDE LINES

- **Fast:** Silkscreened reference guidelines make it easy to align fabric
- **Flexible:** Sub-cut shapes in the sizes you need
- **Accurate:** Easily cut diamonds for designs like Lone Star and 8-Point Star

Description	Item #	Die Board	Price
GO! Strip Cutter-1" (½" Finished) 7 Strips **	55052	10" x 24"	$99.99
GO! Strip Cutter-1", 1½", 2" (½", 1", 1½" Finished) 3 Strips ****	55164	6" x 24"	$79.99
GO! Strip Cutter-1¼" (¾" Finished) 7 Strips **	55109	10" x 24"	$99.99
GO! Strip Cutter-1½" (1" Finished) 5 Strips **	55024	10" x 24"	$99.99
GO! Strip Cutter-1¾" (1¼" Finished) 5 Strips **	55083	10" x 24"	$99.99
GO! Strip Cutter-2" (1½" Finished) 4 Strips **	55025	10" x 24"	$89.99
GO! Strip Cutter-2¼" (1¾" Finished) 4 Strips **	55053	10" x 24"	$89.99
GO! Strip Cutter-2½" (2" Finished) 3 Strips **	55017	10" x 24"	$89.99
GO! Strip Cutter-2½" (2" Finished) 2 Strips ****	55014	6" x 24"	$79.99
GO! Strip Cutter-3" (2½" Finished) 3 Strips **	55084	10" x 24"	$89.99
GO! Strip Cutter-3½" (3" Finished) 2 Strips **	55032	10" x 24"	$89.99
GO! Strip Cutter-4" (3½" Finished) 2 Strips **	55085	10" x 24"	$89.99
GO! Strip Cutter-4½" (4" Finished) 2 Strips **	55054	10" x 24"	$89.99
GO! Strip Cutter-5" (4½" Finished) 1 Strip **	55023	10" x 24"	$89.99
GO! Strip Cutter-5½" (5" Finished) 1 Strip **	55026	10" x 24"	$89.99
GO! Strip Cutter-6½" (6" Finished) 1 Strip **	55086	10" x 24"	$89.99

Compatible with GO! Big® ✱ GO!® ✱ GO! Baby® ✱ GO! Me™ ✱

Use the angled guide lines to cut diamonds.

Subcut perfect squares on the 90° guide line.

GO! Strip Star Sampler Quilt (45" x 45"): Fabric provided by Riley Blake Designs. Download pattern at accuquilt.com

ONE DIE WONDERS.

Block on Board® (BOB®) dies contain all the shapes you need to create a quilt block on a single die. Now you don't even have to think about what shapes are needed to make a block, just cut and GO!

NEW

GO! Bear's Paw-✶✶✶✶
14" Finished 55461 — 6" x 24"
$69.99
Makes 14" finished blocks.

NEW

GO! Cleopatra's Fan-✶✶
12" Finished 55490 — 10" x 24"
$99.99
Makes 14" finished blocks.

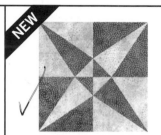

NEW

GO! Crossed Canoes-✶✶
9" Finished 55181 — 10" x 10"
$49.99
Makes 9" finished blocks.

NEW

GO! Pineapple-✶✶✶✶
10" Finished 55485 — 6" x 24"
$79.99
Makes 10" finished blocks.

NEW

GO! Spider Web-✶✶✶✶
6" Finished 55487 — 5" x 10"
$49.99
Makes 12" finished blocks.

GO! Blazing Star-✶✶
6" Finished by Eleanor Burns
55051 — 10" x 10"
$69.99
Makes 12" finished blocks.

GO! Bowties-✶✶✶✶
4" Finished by Alex Anderson
55413 — 6" x 12"
$59.99
Makes 4" finished blocks.

GO! Churn Dash-✶✶
9" Finished 55339 — 10" x 10"
$59.99
Makes 9" finished blocks.

GO! Double Wedding Ring-✶✶
11½" Finished (2-Die Set)
55078 — 10" x 10"
$99.99
Makes 11½" finished blocks.

GO! Dresden Plates-✶✶
55071 — 10" x 24"
$99.99
Use 20 rounded or pointed plates to create full circle; circles are 4" each.

GO! Drunkard's Path-✶✶✶✶
3½" Finished 55070 — 6" x 12"
$49.99
Makes 7" finished blocks.

GO! Drunkard's Path-✶✶
4" Finished 55338 — 10" x 10"
$59.99
Makes 8" finished blocks.

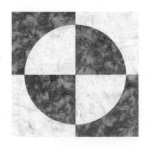

GO! Drunkard's Path-✶✶
7" Finished 55034 — 10" x 24"
$69.99
Makes 14" finished blocks.

GO! Flowering Snowball-✶✶
12" Finished 55252 – 10" x 24"
$89.99
Makes 12" finished blocks.

GO! Hunter Star-✶✶✶✶
6" Finished 55166 – 6" x 12"
$59.99
Makes 12" finished blocks.

GO! Kite-✶✶✶✶
4" Finished 55254 – 6" x 12"
$49.99
Makes 8" finished blocks.

GO! LeMoyne Star-✶✶
9" Finished 55453 – 10" x 10"
$59.99
Makes 9" finished blocks.

GO! Local Color-✶✶✶✶
by Bill Kerr 55452 – 6" x 24"
$79.99
Creates 6" x 12" finished blocks.

GO! Log Cabin-✶✶
12" Finished by Leslie Main 55349 – 10" x 24"
$109.99
Makes 12" finished blocks.

GO! Ohio Star-✶✶✶✶
12" Finished 55174 – 6" x 12"
$49.99
Makes 12" finished blocks.

GO! Rob Peter to Pay Paul-✶✶
7" Finished (2-Die Set) 55068 – 10" x 10"
$79.99
Makes 7" finished blocks.

GO! Snowball-✶✶
6" Finished 55330 – 10" x 10"
$49.99
Makes 6" finished blocks.

GO! Spool-✶✶✶✶
6" Finished 55180 – 6" x 12"
$49.99
Makes 6" finished blocks.

GO! Winding Ways-✶✶
8" Finished 55069 – 10" x 10"
$59.99
Makes 8" finished blocks.

GO! Wonky Heart-✶✶
6" Finished 55471 – 10" x 10"
$59.99
Makes 6" finished blocks.

GO! Bear Foot Wall Hanging (38" x 38"):
Fabric provided by Island Batik.
Download pattern at accuquilt.com

GO! Big® dies are specifically designed to take advantage of the GO! Big cutter's larger size and are only compatible with the GO! Big Electric Cutter.

GO! Big Electric Cutter shown with GO! Big Circles die (55462), sold separately.

NEW

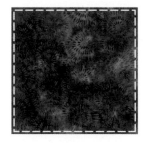

GO! Big Crazy Quilt-*
10" Finished 55861 — 14" x 16"
$99.99
Makes 10" finished blocks.

GO! Big Circle-4", 6", 7", 8"*
55462 — 14" x 16"
$79.99

GO! Big Double Wedding Ring-*
12½" Finished 55258 — 14" x 16"
$99.99
Makes 12½" finished blocks.

GO! Big Square-10"*
(9½" Finished) 55451 — 14" x 16"
$69.99

GO! Big Churn Dash-*
12" Finished 55459 — 14" x 16"
$99.99
Makes 12" finished blocks.

GO! Big Snail's Trail-*
12" Finished 55460 — 14" x 16"
$99.99
Makes 12" finished blocks.

GO! Let's GO Crazy Throw Quilt (40" x 40"):
Download pattern at accuquilt.com

AccuQuilt offers over 200 piecing and appliqué dies designed to cut accurate fabric shapes each and every time, and save time for quilters, so they can get right down to the fun part of quilting!

NEW

GO! Square-1½" ★★★★
(1" Finished) 55470 – 6" x 6"
$34.99

GO! Square-2" ★★★★
(1½" Finished) 55022 – 5" x 10"
$34.99
Makes 6", 9" & 12" finished blocks.

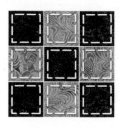

GO! Square-2½" ★★
(2" Finished) Multiples 55059 – 10" x 10"
$59.99
Makes 6", 8" & 12" finished blocks.

use on point

GO! Square on Point-2⅝" ★★★★
(2⅛" Finished) 55394 – 5" x 10"
$34.99
Makes 6" finished blocks.

GO! Square-2¾" ★★★★
(2¼" Finished) 55395 – 5" x 10"
$34.99
Makes 9" finished blocks.

GO! Square-3" ★★★★
(2½" Finished) 55256 – 5" x 10"
$34.99
Makes 10" finished blocks.

use on point

GO! Square on Point-3¼" ★★★★
(2¾" Finished) 55317 – 5" x 10"
$34.99
Makes 8" finished blocks.

GO! Square-3½" ★★★★
(3" Finished) 55006 – 5" x 10"
$34.99
Makes 6", 9" & 12" finished blocks.

use on point

GO! Square on Point- ★★★★
3¹¹⁄₁₆" (3³⁄₁₆" Finished) 55106 – 6" x 12"
$34.99
Makes 9" finished blocks.

GO! Value Die Sampler Quilt (48" x 48"):
Fabric provided by Robert Kaufman Fabrics.
Download pattern at accuquilt.com

4" finished
2" finished
2" finished

GO! Value Die- ★★★★
55018 – 6" x 12"
$39.99
Makes 6", 8" & 12" finished blocks.
Included in GO! Starter Set (55100S).

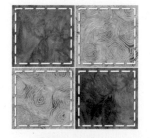

GO! Square-4½" ★★
(4" Finished) Multiples 55060 – 10" x 10"
$59.99
Makes 6", 8" & 12" finished blocks.

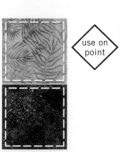

use on point

GO! Square on Point-4¾" ★★★★
(4¼" Finished) 55019 – 6" x 12"
$34.99
Makes 12" finished blocks.

GO! Square-5" ✱✱✱✱
(4½" Finished) 55010 – 6" x 12"
$39.99
Makes 9" finished blocks.

GO! Square-6½" ✱✱
(6" Finished) 55000 – 10" x 10"
$44.99
Makes 6", 8", 9" & 12" finished blocks.

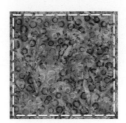

GO! Square-8½" ✱✱
(8" Finished) 55058 – 10" x 10"
$44.99
Makes 8" & 12" finished blocks.

GO! Flying Geese- ✱✱✱✱
3½" x 6½" (3" x 6" Finished) 55456 – 6" x 12"
$39.99
Makes 12" finished blocks.
Included in GO! Big Starter Set (55500).

GO! Half Square Triangle- ✱✱✱✱
1" Finished Square 55320 – 5" x 10"
$34.99
Makes 6", 8", 9" & 12" finished blocks.

GO! Half Square Triangle- ✱✱✱✱
1½" Finished Square 55319 – 5" x 10"
$34.99
Makes 6", 9" & 12" finished blocks.

GO! Half Square Triangle- ✱✱
2" Finished Square-Multiples 55063 – 10" x 10"
$59.99
Makes 6", 8" & 12" finished blocks.

GO! Half Square Triangle- ✱✱✱✱
2¼" Finished Square 55147 – 6" x 12"
$39.99
Makes 9" finished blocks.

GO! Half Square Triangle- ✱✱✱✱
2½" Finished Square 55257 – 5" x 10"
$39.99
Makes 10" finished blocks.

GO! Half Square Triangle- ✱✱✱✱
3" Finished Square 55009 – 5" x 10"
$39.99
Makes 6", 9" & 12" finished blocks.

GO! Half Square Triangle- ✱✱✱✱
4" Finished Square 55031 – 6" x 12"
$44.99
Makes 6", 8" & 12" finished blocks.

GO! Half Square Triangle- ✱✱✱✱
4½" Finished Square 55397 – 6" x 6"
$29.99
Makes 9" finished blocks.

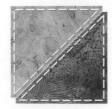

GO! Half Square Triangle- ✱✱
6" Finished Square 55001 – 10" x 10"
$44.99
Makes 6", 8", 9" & 12" finished blocks.

GO! Half Square Triangle- ✱✱
8" Finished Square 55400 – 10" x 24"
$89.99
Makes 8" & 12" finished blocks.

GO! Half Rectangle Triangle- ✱✱✱✱
3" x 6" Finished Rectangle 55411 – 6" x 12"
$39.99
Makes 12" finished blocks.

GO! Quarter Square Triangle- ✱✱✱✱
2" Finished Square 55393 – 5" x 10"
$34.99
Makes 6", 8" & 12" finished blocks.

GO! Quarter Square Triangle-✶✶✶✶
3" Finished Square 55396 – 6" x 12"
$44.99
Makes 6", 9" & 12" finished blocks.

GO! Quarter Square Triangle-✶✶✶✶
4" Finished Square by Alex Anderson
55047 – 6" x 12"
$59.99
Makes 6", 8" & 12" finished blocks.

GO! Quarter Square Triangle-✶✶✶✶
4" Finished Square 55316 – 6" x 12"
$39.99
Makes 6", 8", & 12" finished blocks.

GO! Quarter Square Triangle-✶✶✶✶
4½" Finished Square 55398 – 6" x 12"
$39.99
Makes 9" finished blocks.

GO! Quarter Square Triangle-✶✶✶✶
6" Finished Square 55002 – 6" x 12"
$39.99
Makes 6", 8", 9" & 12" finished blocks.

GO! Quarter Square Triangle-✶✶✶✶
8" Finished Square 55399 – 6" x 24"
$59.99
Makes 8" & 12" finished blocks.

GO! Rectangle-2" x 3½"✶✶✶✶
(1½" x 3" Finished) 55158 – 6" x 6"
$29.99
Makes 6", 9" & 12" finished blocks.

GO! Rectangle-2½" x 4½"✶✶✶✶
(2" x 4" Finished) 55159 – 6" x 12"
$34.99
Makes 8" & 12" finished blocks.

GO! Rectangle-2¾" x 5"✶✶✶✶
(2¼" x 4½" Finished) 55107 – 6" x 12"
$34.99
Makes 9" finished blocks.

GO! Rectangle-3½" x 6½"✶✶✶✶
(3" x 6" Finished) 55005 – 5" x 10"
$34.99
Makes 9" & 12" finished blocks.

GO! Rectangle-4½" x 8½"✶✶
(4" x 8" Finished) 55160 – 10" x 10"
$39.99
Makes 8" & 12" finished blocks.

GO! Parallelogram 45°-2¼" x 2¹³/₁₆"✶✶✶✶
Sides (1½" x 2⅛" Finished) 55402 – 5" x 10"
$34.99
Makes 6" finished blocks.

GO! Parallelogram 45°-✶✶✶✶
2¾" x 3½" Sides
(2¹/₁₆" x 2¹³/₁₆" Finished) 55318 – 5" x 10"
$34.99
Makes 8" finished blocks.

GO! Parallelogram 45°-✶✶✶✶
2¹⁵/₁₆" x 3⅞" Sides
(2¼" x 3³/₁₆" Finished) 55148 – 6" x 12"
$39.99
Makes 9" finished blocks.

GO! Parallelogram 45°-✶✶✶✶
3¹¹/₁₆" x 4¹⁵/₁₆" Sides
(3" x 4¼" Finished) 55004 – 5" x 10"
$34.99
Makes 12" finished blocks.

GO! Diamond 60°-4" Sides✶✶✶✶
(3½" Finished) 55040 – 6" x 12"
$39.99
30° small angle.

GO! Qube 6" Storm at Sea Throw Quilt (50" x 50"):
Fabric provided by Island Batik.
Download pattern at accuquilt.com

GO! Triangle-Isosceles-5" x 6"★★
(4¼" x 5⅛" Finished)
55016 – 10" x 10"
$44.99

GO! Triangles in Square-★★★★
2" Finished Square 55410 – 6" x 6"
$29.99
Makes 6", 8" & 12" finished blocks.

GO! Triangles in Square-★★★★
3" Finished Square 55027 – 6" x 12"
$44.99
Makes 6", 9" & 12" finished blocks.

GO! Triangles in Square-★★★★
4" Finished Square 55409 – 6" x 12"
$44.99
Makes 8" & 12" finished blocks.

GO! Hexagon-1", 1½", 2½" Sides★★★★
(¾", 1¼", 2¼" Fin.) 55011 – 6" x 12"
$39.99
Use with GO! Equilateral
Triangles (55079).

GO! Half Hexagon-1", 1½", 2½" Sides★★★★
(¾", 1¼", 2¼" Fin.) 55165 – 6" x 12"
$49.99
Use with GO! Equilateral
Triangles (55079).

GO! Equilateral Triangles-★★★★
1", 1½", 2½" Sides (¾", 1¼", 2¼" Fin.)
55079 – 6" x 12"
$39.99
Use with GO! Hexagon (55011) and
GO! Half Hexagons (55165).

GO! Island Star Quilt (60" x 60"):
Download pattern at accuquilt.com

GO! Hexagon-4½"★★
Sides (4¼" Finished) 55438 – 10" x 10"
$49.99
Use with GO! Equilateral
Triangle (55429).

GO! Half Hexagon-4½"★★★★
Sides (4¼" Finished) 55437 – 5" x 10"
$34.99
Use with GO! Equilateral
Triangle (55429).

GO! Equilateral Triangle-★★★★
4½" Sides (4¼" Finished) 55429 – 6" x 6"
$29.99
Use with GO! Hexagon-4½"
Sides (55438) and GO! Half Hexagon
(55437).

GO! Apple Core-✷✷✷✷
55036 – 6" x 12"
$39.99
6¼" finished size.

GO! Chisels-✷✷✷✷
55039 – 6" x 12"
$39.99
3" x 6" finished size.

GO! Clamshell-✷✷✷✷
4" Finished 55435 – 6" x 6"
$29.99

GO! Clamshell-✷✷
8" Finished 55436 – 10" x 10"
$49.99

GO! English Paper Piecing Hexagon-½"
Finished Sides✷✷✷✷
55420 – 5" x 10"
$44.99
Cuts fabric and paper.

GO! English Paper Piecing Hexagon-1"
Finished Sides✷✷✷✷
55422 – 6" x 12"
$49.99
Cuts fabric and paper.

GO! Signature Block-✷✷✷✷
4½" Finished 55356 – 5" x 10"
$34.99
Use with GO! Half Square-3" Finished
Triangle (55009).

GO! Wedge-9" Finished✷✷✷✷
55439 – 6" x 12"
$39.99
Use 40 wedges to create
38" full circle.

GO! Tumbler-3½"✷✷✷✷
(3" Finished) 55015 – 6" x 12"
$39.99

GO! Tumbler-4½"✷✷✷✷
(4" Finished) 55445 – 6" x 6"
$29.99

GO! Tumbler-6½"✷✷
(6" Finished) 55020 – 10" x 10"
$49.99

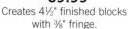

GO! Rag Circle-6½"✷✷
by Heather Banks 55170 – 10" x 10"
$69.99
Creates 4½" finished blocks
with ⅜" fringe.

Dog-eared
Corners!

GO! Rag Square-5¼" ✷✷✷✷
55033 – 6" x 12"
$69.99
3¼" finished size. ¾" fringe. Cut batting
squares with GO! Square-3¼" (55317).

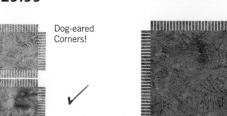

GO! Rag Square-8½" ✷✷
55013 – 10" x 10"
$59.99
6½" finished size. ¾" fringe.
Cut batting squares with
GO! Square-6½" (55000).

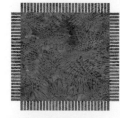

**GO! Christmas Candy Apples
Table Runner** (43¼" x 15½"):
Download pattern at accuquilt.com

GO! Coming Up Roses-★★★★
by Michelle Griffith 55150 – 5" x 10"
$44.99
Bud ¹⁵/₁₆" x ⅞", Roses range 1³/₈"H to 2¹³/₁₆"H;
Leaves range ⁹/₁₆"H to 1½"H. Coordinates
with Michelle's Designs CDs, pg. 33.

GO! Crazy Petals-★★★★
55326 – 6" x 6"
$29.99
Petals 1³/₈" x 2¼", ½" x 1⅛", ¾" x 1¾",
Circles 1⅛", ½", ¾"

GO! Daisy-★★★★
55327 – 6" x 6"
$29.99
4½" and 3⁷/₁₆" assembled sizes.

GO! Fantasy Flowers-★★★★
by Robbi Joy Eklow 55381 – 6" x 24"
$89.99
12³/₈" x 13" assembled size.

GO! Qube 6" Rick Rack Flower Throw Quilt (46" x 46"):
Fabric provided by Timeless Treasures.
Download pattern at accuquilt.com

GO! Feathers-★★★★
55008 – 5" x 10"
$39.99
1³/₈" x 2⁷/₁₆"; 1⁷/₁₆" x 2¾".

GO! Flower-★★★★
55446 – 6" x 6"
$29.99
3½" x 3⁷/₈".

GO! Flower Bunch-★★★★
55332 – 5" x 10"
$39.99
Flowers 1⁷/₈"H to 3½"H;
Leaf ¾"W x 2¼"H; Flower Center ¾".

GO! Flower Power-★★★★
by Sarah Vedeler 55309 – 6" x 12"
$49.99
Circle 4"; Petals 1⅛" x 2¼",
1⁷/₈" x 3⁷/₈", 2⁷/₈" x 6".

GO! Fun Flower-★★★★
55334 – 6" x 6"
$29.99
4½" x 4¼".

GO! Funky Flowers-★★★★
55042 – 5" x 10"
$39.99
4" x 4⅛" assembled sizes.

GO! Grapes of Wrath-★★★★
by Alex Anderson 55370 – 5" x 10"
$39.99
5½" x 5⁵⁄₁₆" assembled size.

Stem not
included
(Use 55331)

GO! Harrison Rose-★★
by Eleanor Burns 55403 – 10" x 24"
$109.99
Makes 14" finished blocks. Flower 9".

GO! Orange Peel-4½"-★★★★
55455 – 6" x 6"
$29.99
Makes 9" finished blocks.
Use with GO! Square-5" (55010).

GO! Pomegranate-★★★★
by Alex Anderson 55371 – 5" x 10"
$39.99
Circles 2½", 3¼";
Cat's Eyes range 2⁵⁄₁₆"H to 2¹⁵⁄₁₆"H;
Leaves range 3"H to 3¾"H.

GO! Ring of Oak-★★★★
by Stacy Michell 55378 – 5" x 10"
$44.99
9⁷⁄₁₆" x 9¼" assembled size.

GO! Rose of Sharon #1-★★★★
by Sharon Pederson 55045 – 5" x 10"
$59.99
Roses 1", 1½", 2", 2½", 3".

GO! Rose of Sharon #2-★★
by Sharon Pederson 55382 – 10" x 10"
$69.99
Roses 3½", 4", 4½", 5".

GO! Round Flower-★★★★
55007 – 5" x 10"
$39.99
3½" x 8½" assembled size.

GO! Simple Shapes by Edyta Sitar-★★★★
55177 – 6" x 12"
$69.99
Bird 2⅞" x 2¾"; Buds range 2¼"H to 3"H;
Leaves range 1¾"H to 4¾"H; Stem 1"W x
10"H; Centers ⅝", 1", 1¾".

GO! Stems & Leaves-★★★★
55331 – 6" x 12"
$49.99
Stems approx. 7½"H. Leaves range
from 1½"H to 3½"H.

GO! Harrison Rose Wall Hanging
by Eleanor Burns (60" x 60"):
Download pattern at accuquilt.com

GO! Tulip-★★★★
55328 – 6" x 6"
$29.99
4¾" x 4¼" assembled size.

APPLY FUSIBLE WEB

to the wrong side of
fabric, then cut with
your favorite shape.

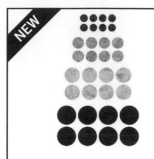

NEW

GO! Circle-½", ¾", 1", 1¼" ★★★★
55484 — 6" x 12"
$59.99*

GO! Circle-1½", 1¾", 2¼", 2½" ★★★★
55155 — 6" x 12"
$49.99

GO! Circle-2", 3", 5" ★★★★
55012 — 6" x 12"
$44.99

GO! Circle-6" ★★
55384 — 10" x 10"
$44.99

GO! Circle-8" ★★
55360 — 10" x 10"
$44.99

GO! Fleur De Lis- ★★★★
55345 — 6" x 6"
$29.99
4¼"W x 5"H.

GO! Heart-2", 3", 4" ★★★★
55029 — 5" x 10"
$39.99

GO! Queen of Hearts- ★★★★
55325 — 6" x 12"
$49.99
Hearts range 2"W x 1⅜"H
to 4"W x 3"H.

GO! Star-2", 3", 4" ★★★★
55028 — 5" x 10"
$39.99

GO! Star-8 Point- ★★★★
by Sarah Vedeler 55315 — 6" x 12"
$49.99
Stars 5" and 3½" point to point;
Petal 1⅜" x 4½".

GO! Star Points- ★★★★
by Sarah Vedeler 55314 — 5" x 10"
$39.99
5 Point Petal 2½" x 5";
6 Point Petal 3" x 5".

GO! Sparkle-Diamonds- ★★★★
by Sarah Vedeler 55089 — 6" x 12"
$59.99
Small 1" x 2½"; Medium 1⅝" x 4";
Large 3¼" x 8".

GO! Heather Feather #1- ★★★★
by Sarah Vedeler 55087 — 6" x 12"
$69.99
8¾" x 11¼" assembled size.

GO! Heather Feather #2- ★★★★
by Sarah Vedeler 55088 — 6" x 12"
$69.99
6⅜" x 10⅞" assembled size.

GO! Heather Feather Border- ★★★★
Collection by Sarah Vedeler 55414 — 6" x 24"
$109.99
32", 48", 64" or 80" assembled sizes.

CREATE QUILTS

you never thought
you would — AccuQuilt
makes cutting curvy
classic quilt patterns
a snap.

GO! Carefree Alphabet Uppercase Set-★★
(2-Die Set) 55092 – 10" x 24"
$199.99*
Letters are 3" tall.

NEW

GO! Carefree Alphabet Lowercase Set-★★
(2-Die Set) 55491 – 10" x 24"
$199.99*
Letters are 3" tall.

GO! Carefree Numbers-★★
55099 – 10" x 10"
$69.99*
Numbers are 3" tall.

GO! Peace by Sarah Vedeler-★★
55305 – 10" x 10"
$79.99
Letters 4½" tall.

GO! Love by Sarah Vedeler-★★
55306 – 10" x 10"
$79.99
Letters 4½" tall.

GO! Joy by Sarah Vedeler-★★★★
55307 – 6" x 12"
$59.99
Letters 4½" tall,

GO! Ribbon Twist-★★★★
55055 – 6" x 12"
$59.99

GO! Rick Rack-★★★★
55056 – 6" x 24"
$69.99
Wide 23" x 4", Narrow 23" x 2".
No blades on ends.

GO! Scallop Border-★★★★
55417 – 6" x 24"
$79.99
Width of the strip can vary.

GO! Swag by Alex Anderson-★★★★
55108 – 6" x 24"
$89.99
Scalloped swag 12"W x ⅞"D;
Crescent swag 12"W x 2½"D.

GO! Swirling Bubbles (28" x 28"):
Download pattern at accuquilt.com

GO! Rustling Leaves #1-★★★★
55389 – 5" x 10"
$44.99
3½" x 4", 4" x 3⅝".

GO! Rustling Leaves #2-★★★★
55390 – 5" x 10"
$44.99
4" x 3½", 3¼" x 5⅛".

GO! Rustling Leaves #3-★★★★
55391 – 6" x 6"
$34.99
3⅛" x 2⅜", 3⅛" x 2⅞".

GO! Rustling Leaves #4-★★★★
55392 – 6" x 6"
$34.99
3⅛" x 2¾", 2⅝" x 4⅛".

GO! Quilted Leaves and Logs Wall Hanging (40" x 40"):
Fabric provided by Robert Kaufman Fabrics.
Download pattern at accuquilt.com

GO! Fall Medley-★★★★
55041 – 6" x 12"
$49.99
Shapes range 4"H to 5"H.

GO! Pumpkins-★★★★
55323 – 6" x 12"
$49.99
Pumpkins range 3"H to 4½"H.

GO! Cat & Bat-★★★★
55365 – 6" x 12"
$49.99
Cat 5⅛" x 7⅜", Bat 5⅛" x 3".

GO! Bohemia #1 by Ricky Tims★★★★
55368 – 6" x 12"
$59.99
8½" x 7¼" assembled size.

GO! Arabesque #1 by Ricky Tims-★★
55046 – 10" x 10"
$79.99
3¾" x 3"; 8½" x 4¼"; 10⅛" x 5".

GO! Arabesque #2 by Ricky Tims-★★
55049 – 10" x 10"
$69.99
7⅛" x 7⅛".

GO! Arabesque #3 by Ricky Tims-★★
55050 – 10" x 10"
$69.99
8⅜" x 8⅜".

55364 & 55368
assembled

GO! Bohemia #2 by Ricky Tims-★★★★
55364 – 6" x 24"
$79.99
26½" x 61³⁄₁₆" assembled size.
Use with Bohemia #1 (55368).

GO! Angel-✶✶✶✶
55418 – 6" x 12"
$69.99
6" x 6¾" assembled size.

GO! Holiday Accessories-✶✶✶✶
55321 – 6" x 12"
$49.99
Use with GO! Circle-2" 3" 5" (55012).

GO! Reindeer-✶✶✶✶
55353 – 6" x 6"
$29.99
4¾" x 4⅜".

GO! Sleigh & Snowflakes-✶✶
55322 – 10" x 10"
$59.99
Shapes range 4"H to 5"H.

GO! Holiday Medley-✶✶✶✶
55043 – 6" x 12"
$49.99
Holly 2" x 3¼"; Berries ½";
Tree & Snowflake are 5" tall.

GO! Snowflakes-7" ✶✶✶✶
55450 – 10" x 24"
$109.99
6¼" x 7", 6⅜" x 7", 6⅝" x 7",

GO! Snowflake-✶✶✶✶
55359 – 6" x 6"
$29.99
3⅝" x 4".

GO! Sparkle-Snowflakes-✶✶✶✶
by Sarah Vedeler 55093 – 6" x 12"
$49.99
12 Point 4½" x 4⅞"; 6 Point 4¼" x 5".

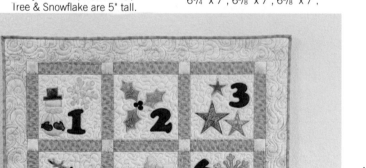

GO! 12 Days of Winter Bliss Wall Hanging (40" x 48"):
Download pattern at accuquilt.com

GO! Sparkle-Tree-✶✶
by Sarah Vedeler 55095 – 10" x 10"
$69.99
36" x 48½" assembled size.

GO! Bow-2½", 3½", 4½" ✶✶✶✶
55341 – 6" x 12"
$49.99
2½"W x 1⅞"H, 3½"W x 2⅝"H,
4½"W x 3½"H.

GO! Sparkle-Slim Tree-✶✶
by Sarah Vedeler 55096 – 10" x 10"
$69.99
Assembled: Large Tree 4¼" x 13⅛";
Small Tree 2⅛" x 6½"

GO! Sparkle-Jumbo Tree-✶✶✶✶
by Sarah Vedeler 55094 – 6" x 12"
$59.99
Concave 2¼" x 1⅞";
Convex 2⅜" x 1⅞".

GO! Appliqué Fabric Cutting Dies

GO! Qube 8" Sunbonnet Sue Bows Quilt (52" x 66"):
Fabric provided by QT Fabrics.
Download pattern at accuquilt.com

GO! Sunbonnet Sue-★★★★
55061 – 5" x 10"
$39.99*
5³⁄₈" x 7¹⁄₂" assembled size.

GO! Overall Sam-★★★★
55062 – 5" x 10"
$39.99
4¹⁄₂" x 8¹⁄₂" assembled size.

GO! Cupcake-★★★★
55097 – 6" x 12"
$49.99
3⁷⁄₈" x 4¹⁄₂", 4¹⁄₄" x 5"
assembled sizes.

GO! Dancing Umbrella-★★★★
by Edyta Sitar 55178 – 6" x 12"
$49.99
8³⁄₄" x 9³⁄₈" assembled size.

GO! Home by Stacy Michell-★★★★
55379 – 6" x 12"
$59.99
5¹⁄₂" x 6¹⁄₂" assembled size.

GO! Schoolhouse-★★
55344 – 10" x 10"
$59.99
9¹⁄₂"W x 8"H assembled size.

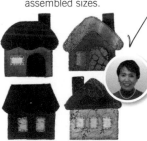

GO! Small Houses-★★★★
by Reiko Kato 55387 – 6" x 12"
$59.99
Houses range 2⁵⁄₈"H to 3¹⁄₂"H.

GO! Trees by Reiko Kato-★★★★
55388 – 6" x 6"
$39.99
Approx. 3"H to 3³⁄₈"H assembled.

NEW

GO! Music Medley-★★★★
55482 – 6" x 12"
$59.99*
Shapes range 3¹⁄₈"H to 5⁷⁄₁₆"H.

GO! Awareness Ribbon-★★★★
55355 – 6" x 6"
$29.99
2¹⁄₂" x 5".

GO! Eagle by Eleanor Burns-★★
55383 – 10" x 10"
$69.99
16⁹⁄₁₆" x 9¹⁄₄" assembled size.

GO! Folk Art Fowl by Bill Kerr-★★★★
55375 – 6" x 12"
$59.99
Rooster 5⁷⁄₁₆"H; Hen 4³⁄₄"H;
Eggs 1³⁄₄"H.

10th ANNIVERSARY LIMITED-EDITION DIE

GO! Airplanes ★★★★
55366 – 6" x 12"
$59.99*
Plane 4⅛" x 4¼"; Bi-Plane 5⅛" x 3⅛".

GO! Cute Car ★★★★
55354 – 5" x 10"
$39.99
5½" x 3⅜".

GO! Train ★★★★
55367 – 6" x 24"
$69.99
Shapes range 4¾"W to 5⅝"W.

GO! Owl ★★★★
55333 – 6" x 6"
$34.99
4"W x 4½"H assembled size.

GO! Birds ★★★★
55324 – 6" x 12"
$49.99
Birds range 2¾"H to 3⁷⁄₁₆"H.

GO! Baby, Baby ★★★★
55037 – 5" x 10"
$39.99
Shapes are 4" tall.

GO! Lullaby ★★★★
55038 – 6" x 12"
$39.99
Rattle: 2½" to 5";
Sheep: 4⅛" to 3⁵⁄₁₆"

NEW

GO! Spring Medley ★★★★
55494 – 6" x 12"
$49.99*
Chick 3½" x 4½", Basket 3⅞" x 4½",
Egg 1¼" x 1¹¹⁄₁₆"; Bunny 4½" x 3½"

GO! Bird ★★★★
55352 – 6" x 6"
$29.99
3³⁄₈" x 3¾".

GO! Cardinal ★★★★
55351 – 6" x 6"
$29.99
4³⁄₈" x 4½".

QUICK & EASY APPLIQUÉ

apply fusible web to fabric prior to cutting.

GO! Dove ★★★★
55350 – 6" x 6"
$29.99
4⁷⁄₈" x 4½".

GO! Spring Medley Table Runner (32" x 12"):
Download pattern at accuquilt.com

10th ANNIVERSARY LIMITED-EDITION DIE

GO! Leaping Frog-★★★★
55199 – 6" x 6"
$34.99*
4⁹⁄₁₆" x 5".

NEW

GO! Northwoods Medley-★★★★
55483 – 6" x 12"
$59.99*
Shapes range 4⁷⁄₈"H x 5⅛"H.

10th ANNIVERSARY LIMITED-EDITION DIE

GO! Elephants-★★★★
55373 – 5" x 10"
$44.99*
Large 4½" x 4"; Small 3⁷⁄₁₆" x 2⁵⁄₁₆".

GO! Zoo Animals-★★★★
55369 – 6" x 12"
$59.99
Monkey 3⅛" x 2⅞"; Lion 4⅞" x 4⅛";
Giraffe 4⅝" x 6½".

GO! Wild in Northwoods Quilt (28" x 28"):
Fabric provided by Island Batik.
Download pattern at accuquilt.com

GO! Elephant Carousel Quilt (36" x 36"):
Download pattern at accuquilt.com

GO! Calico Cat-★★★★
55065 – 6" x 6"
$29.99
3³⁄₁₆" x 4½".

GO! Gingham Dog-★★★★
55064 – 6" x 6"
$29.99
4½" x 3⅞" assembled size.

GO! Butterfly-★★★★
by Edyta Sitar 55467 – 5" x 10"
$49.99
8"W x 7½"H assembled size.

GO! Critters-★★★★
55030 – 6" x 12"
$49.99
Shapes are 4" tall.

MACHINE EMBROIDERY DESIGNS BY MARJORIE BUSBY

Marjorie Busby of Blue Feather Quilt Studio has created a wonderful collection of Machine Embroidery Designs for use with AccuQuilt GO! Wide range of file formats.

GO!® Birds CD
MBME55324 $21⁰⁰

GO!® Critters CD
MBME55030 $18⁰⁰

GO!® Cute Car CD
MBME55354 $24⁰⁰

GO!® Fall Medley CD
MBME55041 $18⁰⁰

GO!® Fun Flower CD
MBME55334 $15⁰⁰

GO!® Holiday Medley CD
MBME55043 $21⁰⁰

GO!® Home CD
MBME55379 $21⁰⁰

GO!® Overall Sam CD
MBME55062 $21⁰⁰

GO!® Sunbonnet Sue CD
MBME55061 $21⁰⁰

GO!® Winter Bliss CD
MBME10185 $21⁰⁰

GO!® Zoo Animals CD
MBME55369 $21⁰⁰

File formats: ART, dst, exp, hus, jef, pes, sew, vip, vp3

MACHINE EMBROIDERY DESIGN BY MICHELLE'S DESIGNS

Coming Up Roses CD
3760 $59⁹⁵

More Coming Up Roses CD
3766 $59⁹⁵

Through the Garden CD
3753 $59⁹⁵

PATTERN BOOKS FOR GO!®

You'll love these pattern books written to coordinate with GO!® dies. Books feature a variety of patterns for beginner to intermediate quilters to choose from.

GO!® Qube™ by Eleanor Burns
1091 $24⁹⁵

Wearables on the GO!®
55939 $16⁹⁹

GO! Baby® Quilting –
Small Quilts & Novelties
55983 $16⁹⁹

Quilting on the GO!®
DO5356 $18⁹⁹

Rainy Day Tea Time by Edyta Sitar
11329 $15⁹⁵

GO!® CUTTING MATS

Specially formulated cutting mats are part of the precision system that makes the AccuQuilt GO!® fabric cutters and dies so efficient. Choose a mat that matches the die board size you are using and get cutting with ease!

Cutting Mat-6" x 6"
$9.99 55137

Cutting Mat-6" x 6"
(2-pack)
$18.99 55139

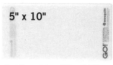

Cutting Mat-5" x 10"
$9.99 55110

Cutting Mat-10" x 10"
$12.99 55111

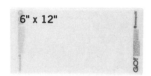

Cutting Mat-6" x 12"
$12.99 55112

Cutting Mat-14" x 16"
$29.99 55146

Cutting Mat-6" x 24"
$18.99 55138

Cutting Mat-10" x 24"
$29.99 55113

GO!® DIE PICK

A must-have tool for proper care and cleaning of GO! dies. Keeping your dies free of threads will produce better cutting results.

$5.99 (55105)

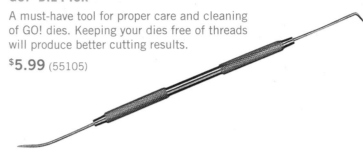

GO!® DIE STORAGE RACK

Easily and conveniently store dies upright in this stylish rack. Holds eight GO! dies and mats of all sizes on the floor or table.

$24.99 (55115)

GO!® FABRIC CUTTER TOTE & DIE BAG

Accessory die bag holds an 18" x 24" rotary cutting mat and GO! strip cutter dies. Select classic black or GO! green.

- Tote: 20"W x 7"L x 16"H
- Tote height with handle fully extended: 43"
- Front Pocket: 18"W x 1"L x 14"H
- Interior compartment: 20"W x 7"L x 15"H
- Die Bag: 20"W x ¾"L x 25"H
- Weight: 9 lbs. (4 kg)

Black
$169.99 (55250)

Green
$169.99 (55251)

PERSONALIZE. ORGANIZE. STORE.

The GO!® Die Storage System is the perfect organizational solution for any quilter. The neutral design fits any décor and the functional design easily stacks on a shelf or counter. There are even labels for personalizing and the ultimate ease of use.

NEW LOW PRICE!

GO!® Die Storage 6" x 6"
Self-contained Storage System for (8) 6" x 6" GO! Dies.

$14.99 (55850)

GO!® Die Storage 6" x 12"
Self-contained Storage System for (8) 6" x 12" GO! Dies or 5" x 10" GO! Dies.

$14.99 (55851)

GO!® Die Storage 10" x 10"
Self-contained Storage System for (4) 10" x 10" GO! Dies.

$14.99 (55852)

AVAILABLE FOR A LIMITED TIME!

GO!® Die Storage Limited-Edition 6" x 12"
Self-contained Storage System for (8) 6" x 12" GO! Dies or 5" x 10" GO! Dies.

$14.99 (55853)

10th ANNIVERSARY

Includes labels for personalizing   (Dies shown not included.)

accuquilt®

8843 S 137th Circle
Omaha, NE 68138
accuquilt.com

Find GO!® products at
retail stores and accuquilt.com.

Fall in love with 5 new GO! dies.

We're excited to introduce five new GO! dies to add to your collection. 3 Block on Board (BOB®) dies and 2 new appliquè dies.

- GO! Carefree Alphabet Lowercase Set (55491)
- GO! Spring Medley (55494)
- GO! Bear's Paw-14" Finished (55461)
- GO! Cleopatra's Fan-12" Finished (55490)
- GO! Big Crazy Quilt-10" Finished (55861)

LEARN MORE ON PAGES 16, 18, 27 & 31.

We can make your CUSTOM DIES

Whether you have a shape you'd like multiples of or a great idea for a new appliqué shape, Custom Shape Pros can create a custom GO! die for you.

1. REQUEST A FREE QUOTE.
2. REVIEW AND APPROVE QUOTE.
3. APPROVE FINAL DRAWING.
4. SHIPS IN 5 BUSINESS DAYS!

Get started today with a free no-obligation quote at CustomShapePros.com

Aquamarine
Ambience

with Jenny Haskins

A new quilt by

Simon G Haskins

First published in USA 2006
by Quilters Resource Inc
Phone: Toll Free 1800 676 6543
Email: **info@quiltersresource.com**

Text, projects, embroidery and photography copyright ' Unique Creative Opportunities 2006

All rights reserved. Without limiting the rights under copyright reserved above,
no part of this publication may be reproduced, stored in or introduced into a retrieval system,
or transmitted, in any form or by any means (electronic, mechanical, photocopying, recording
or otherwise), without the prior written permission of both the copyright owner and the
above publisher of this book.

Text: Jenny Haskins
Quilt by: Simon Haskins
Designer: Suzy King
Photography: Tom Evangelidis and Laurie Haskins
Styling: Jenny Haskins and Robyn Wilson

National Library of Congress
Cataloguing-in-Publication Data applied for

Haskins, Jenny
Haskins, Simon
Aquamarine Ambience

ISBN 1-889682-52-7

Printed in China

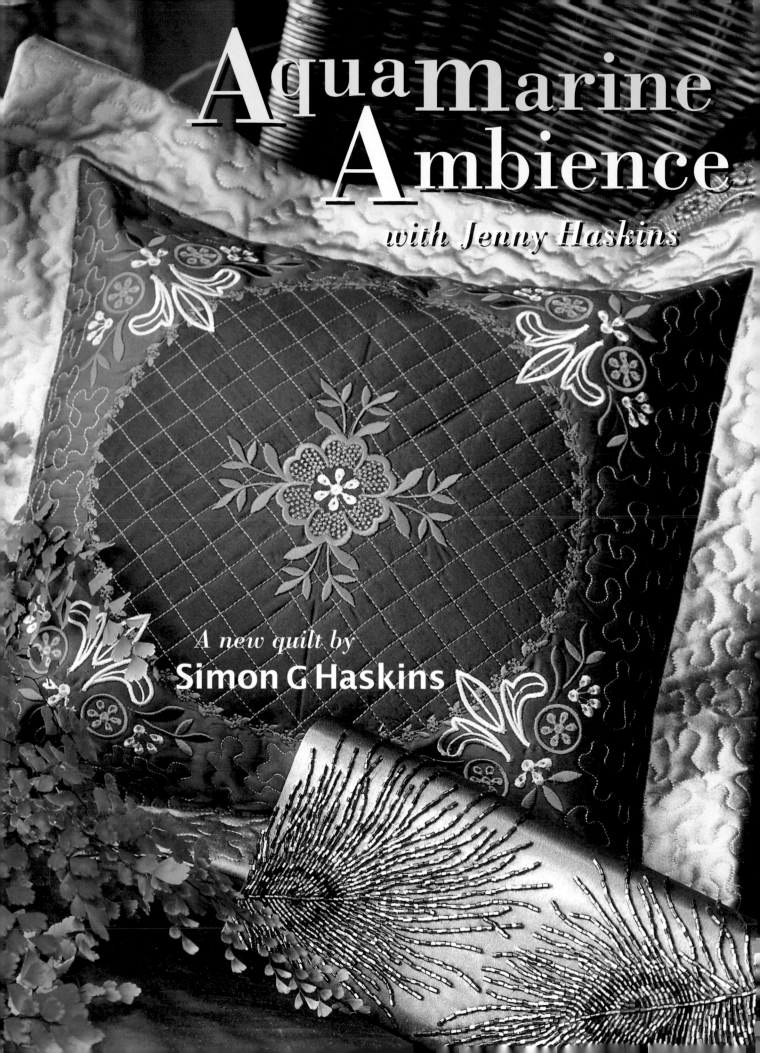

Aquamarine
Ambience

with *Jenny Haskins*

A new quilt by
Simon G Haskins

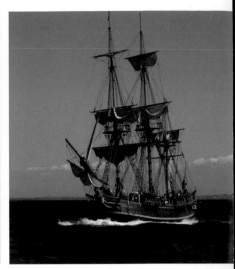

Captain's Log

I have three children. Jason is the eldest, Samantha the youngest, and Simon is in between. Simon is also my partner in Unique Creative Opportunities Pty Limited, the business I started in 1999. UCO produces design CDs, original quilts, books and magazines. Simon has a degree in Economics, Social Science and Psychology from Sydney University, one of Australia's most prestigious campuses. Having won the Maths and Art awards in his final year of high school it is no wonder that once he had received his degree he wanted to explore his creative side.

Travelling around the US for the past five years, Simon has assisted me in teaching, demonstrating and lecturing, and has attended the *Houston Quilt Market and Festival* (his quilts were on display along with mine in 2005 in our Special Exhibition), Martha Pullen's School, Sewing Machine Conventions and numerous teaching events around the world. In all of these he has been my right hand.

Aquamarine Ambience (a quilt made by Simon for his friend Kristina Hickey's 30th birthday) is his second original quilt, following the sell-out success of *Simon's Folly* (Pride Publishing 2005, a *Creative Expressions* Special of the same name). So it is again with considerable pride and excitement that I present his latest quilt to avid machine-embroidery quilters.

*Simon on his 28th birthday 2005
sailing on a tall ship –
he is with you on your voyage on the
sea of* Aquamarine Ambience.

Aquamarine Ambience was inspired by the colors of the sea as they change with the water's depth; one color merges into another as the light reflects off the water, and shadows seem to hover just above its surface. So too do the fabrics, threads and embroidery of this quilt all seem to merge. The colors, texture and luster of the fabrics and threads seem to glisten and shimmer to create a special ambience that an aquamarine sea evokes for so many of us; those whose souls find peace in the sights, sounds and smell of the ocean. As each wave brings its own unique form, movement and color, so too does each block of Simon's quilt.

I have written the instructions for the quilt, along with those for the pillows and table runner (in different color stories) in such a way that even a novice can follow them, and I feel confident sharing the easy tips I have learned over the past 15 years – tips that make machine embroidery and quilting easy and fun yet challenging enough to excite and inspire the most experienced machine-embroiderer or quilter.

As a (totally biased) mother, and as an artist and business person, I would describe Simon as a gifted young man whose many talents and qualities assure him of a brilliant future in any area he should choose. He has so much to offer when it comes to the sewing, quilting and embroidery industries, sharing his special flair and talents with all who come in contact with him.

So come and share our voyage of discovery – set sail with threads, fabric, embroidery designs (free on the accompanying CD) and machine on the sea of *Aquamarine Ambience* – and visit the creative shores of machine-embroidered quilting.

Jerry

Contents

102

22

98

88

Plotting the Course in the Sea of Aquamarine Ambience

The sea has always been where Jenny finds her soul; she finds peace and perception in the sounds of the sea, inspiration in the sparkling colors of the water and cleansing through the salty air. It is no wonder then that this fascination for the sea has been passed on to her son Simon, and is in his heart also.

Aquamarine (a greenish blue color as well as a gemstone reflecting this color) Ambience (meaning mood, feeling or atmosphere) aptly describes Simon's unique quilt, which captures the color and mood of an expanse of ocean, with its crystal clear water and colors that seem to shift with its depth, tide and the breeze. One can almost imagine a mermaid hiding in the shadows of the glistening embroidery designs, as described by Alfred Lord Tennyson.

For those of us who love the sea, it is mesmerising, ever-changing and restless, yet can bring amazing calm. Its many colors and feelings are reflected in *Aquamarine Ambience* – a quilt of changing moods, colors and feelings that reflect Simon's brilliance.

Simon chose nap silk dupione (light and dark green, interwoven with light and dark blue), which reflects the light and the shimmer of the glorious Robison-Anton rayon threads.

This quilt teaches multi-template embroidery (done the easy way), accurate cutting and piecing of circles (using the *Cut A Round* tool that Simon and Jenny discovered in Houston in 2005), as well as cutting and piecing nap fabric so the grain is consistent with the sashing and border fabrics.

Who would be
A mermaid fair,
Singing alone,
Combing her hair
Under the sea,
In a golden curl
With a comb of pearl,
On a throne?

Loading the Cargo
& Training the Crew

Preparation

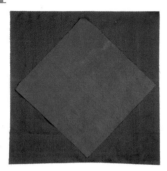

JENNYS TIP: Take time to read and understand this section of the instructions as it will guarantee smooth sailing when you reach the embroidery and construction stages. There is considerable preparation involved in the cutting, inserting the circles, preparing and marking the blocks, so allow yourself uninterrupted time and uncluttered space with plenty of light to eliminate frustration and ensure accuracy.

Cutting

(this is done on a need-to-use basis)

There are three rules of thumb when cutting fabric for quilting:

☀ For a plain fabric, always keep the fabric grain straight.

☀ For a nap fabric, keep the nap of the fabric running in the same direction throughout the quilt; this can mean cutting with or against the grain, depending on where the fabric sits on the quilt when pieced. *Aquamarine Ambience* is made from a nap silk fabric.

☀ Measure twice and cut once.

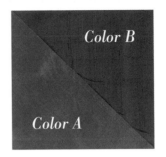

Color B

Color A

1 Use the rotary cutter, self-healing cutting mat and quilter's ruler to cut from:

Color B fabric and the lightweight fusible batting

☀ 12, 18in squares for the background frame fabric (after the embroidery has been done, these will be cut into 15½in squares).

Color A fabric

☀ 12, 12in squares (circle inserts will be cut from these).

JENNY'S TIP: Fold your fabric very accurately to ensure perfect circles.

2 All 24 fabric squares need to be folded into quarters (fourths) by folding the fabric in half on the horizontal and then again on the vertical, so that the raw fabric edges are aligned and parallel

on two sides to form a right angle, and the folded edges are aligned and parallel on the opposite sides to form a right angle. Lightly press each folded square to hold the fold lines.

3 Place the folded fabric squares in two piles according to their fabric and size. Mark the 12in squares 'Color A' for the circle inserts and the 18in squares 'Color B' for the background frame fabric.

JENNY'S TIP: The circles are all cut and joined according to the detailed instructions that come with the Cut A Round tool, so make sure you read and understand how the tool works before cutting the center circles and frame circular holes from the relevant fabric squares.

NOTE: The Inch Rule is: The circular hole in the background fabric is ONE INCH SMALLER than the circle you want to set in.

Color B frame fabric

4 Place the 18in folded fabric square, Color B, on the self-healing cutting mat so the folded corner is at the bottom, the fabric edge corner is on the top, and the corners are matched on a vertical grid line.

5 Place the *Cut A Round* tool centered over the folded Color B fabric so the folded corner is at the bottom and the raw fabric edge corner is at the

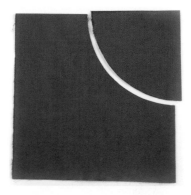

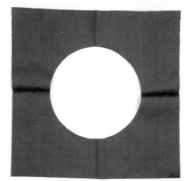

top, matching fabric folds, to corresponding marks on the *Cut A Round* tool. The center vertical line marked on the *Cut A Round* tool should be centered over the fabric running from the bottom folded corner of the fabric to the top raw fabric edged corner of the fabric.

6 Select the 10in line and insert the 45mm rotary cutter in the space provided. Then, holding the rotary cutter erect, cut slowly and deliberately, following the curved channel in the *Cut A Round* tool.

7 Cut all 12, 10in circle holes from the Color B fabric, leave the squares folded and put them to one side. The fabric circles from the center of the square can be used in a future project.

Color A center circles

8 Using the 12in Color A folded squares, repeat Steps 4 to 7, selecting the 11in line, leaving the circles folded and discarding the fabric from around the circle.

Folding fabric frames and circles for piecing

9 Each fabric frame and circle needs to be folded into eighths by taking the two free folds (one over and one under) to meet and align with and be parallel to the fixed fold. Lightly press each one.

Frame

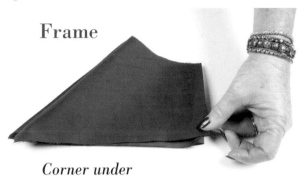

Corner under

Circle

Corner over

10 Unfold both the frame and the circle fabric pieces. Place a pin vertically on the fold lines of one circle and one frame piece of fabric on the circular cut edge.

NOTE: As we are working with nap fabric it is very important to mark the grain on each frame Color B fabric and each circle Color A fabric, so the nap grain on each fabric group is running the same way. When pinning and subsequently stitching the circle to the frame, make sure that the nap grain of Color A fabric circles runs horizontally and the nap grain of Color B

fabric frames runs vertically, then mark the top of each fabric piece. (The nap grain of subsequent cutting of these fabrics will need to be the same; see layout diagram on page 82.)

Piecing the circles and frames

11 Place the fabric circle on a flat surface, right side up, then place the fabric frame over the circle (also right side up), matching and noting the top of the circle Color A fabric and the top of the frame Color B fabric.

12 Bring the outside straight fabric edge of the frame fabric towards the middle of the circle, matching the pins on the frame circle with those of the circle, then pin them together at the folded eighth intervals with the pins placed in the fabric vertically, easing the fabric together between the pins and pinning at intervals.

13 Use the patchwork ¼in foot No 37, construction thread in the Jeans 80 needle and bobbin and a straight stitch length 2. Place the circle on the bed of the sewing machine with the frame fabric under the needle to sew an accurate ¼in seam. The circle will be inserted into the frame with the edge of the foot aligned with and parallel to the raw fabric edges at all times, and concentrating on one section at a time.

14   Use a hot steam iron to press the seam flat towards the center of the inserted circle.

15   Insert circles into the remaining 11 fabric frames for a total of 12, 18in frames inserted with circles (blocks).

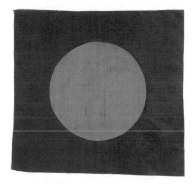

Marking the blocks

JENNY'S TIP: The glue on the back of the fusible batting is a steam- and heat-activated bond. To make sure the batting is totally fused to the back of the fabric, and if your iron does not generate enough steam, you may need to use a light spray of water; the fabric needs to be totally and evenly secured to the batting as if one fabric. If the batting is not secured firmly to the back of the fabric, the fabric will move during embroidery causing the embroidery design to distort and the fabric to pucker.

16   Use a hot steam iron to fuse the 18in lightweight fusible batting square to the back of the 18in silk squares with the inserted circles.

JENNY'S TIP: Correct stabilizing of fabric for embroidery will ensure perfect results, so make sure each coat of spray starch covers the fabric area evenly and is completely dry before applying subsequent layers. Correctly stabilized fabric held securely to batting and hoop stabilizer reduces puckers and embroidery distortion and ensures perfect results.

17   Stabilize each block by using three coats of heavy-duty spray starch, ironing between coats. Note that if you have marked the top of each block with a chalk pencil (to show the nap grain direction), you may need to remark it after stabilizing it with the spray starch.

18   Use the quilter's ruler and Clover chalk pencil to mark the batting-backed blocks with vertical, horizontal and diagonal lines that intersect through the center of each square.

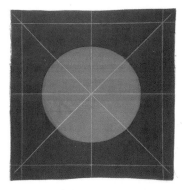

19   Measure out and mark 7½in from the center of each block on the vertical and horizontal lines, then use the quilter's ruler and chalk pencil to draw vertical and horizontal lines that pass through these marks, creating a 15in square inside each block. Place the blocks to one side.

Jenny's Tricks of the Trade

These tips are guaranteed to give even the novice embroiderer perfect results every time, and to teach a more experienced artist how to make an embroidered quilt even easier.

 ## Designs and templates

1   The Bernina Artista design software and transfer device are used to transfer embroidery designs from the *Aquamarine Ambience* design CD that accompanies this book to your computer, then your machine.

2   Go to the Bernina website (**www.berninausa.com**). Select *What's New*, then *FREE Downloads*, then *Free Embroidery Hoop Basting Designs*, then the appropriate hoop size to suit your machine. Now download this to your computer (*Aquamarine Ambience* designs use the 255mm x 145mm oval hoop). Follow the directions found on the website on how to use the basting stitch in conjunction with your embroidery designs.

3   The Bernina Artista design software, a PC and a regular printer are used to print placement templates on vellum tracing paper for all embroidery designs.

4   Use the awl to punch holes on each end of the vertical and horizontal divide lines that intersect the center of the design, and also through the center on each vellum placement template.

See point No 6

5   These placement holes are used when the template is positioned (in the desired place) over the fabric, and then a chalk pencil is used to mark a dot through the punched holes onto the fabric. These dots are then connected using a quilter's ruler and chalk pencil, thus replicating the lines on the template. These lines are used to place embroidery designs with ease and precision and are essential when connecting designs or when one design is made up of several smaller designs. It is also important to mark the top of the hoop for each design, both on the template and the fabric.

See point No 5

6   If two or more embroidery designs are needed to make one large embroidery motif or a combination of embroideries, the templates for each design section are printed, combined and then held together with sticky tape, with positioning holes being punched on each separate embroidery design template. Again, mark the top of the hoop for each design on each template and on the fabric. The positioning holes are marked through onto the fabric with a chalk pencil, and the dots are connected on the fabric for each embroidery or section of an embroidery motif. This then gives the center position (with vertical and horizontal lines marked for keeping the fabric straight on the stabilizer in the hoop) for each section of the design. It is advisable to recheck each section of the design before commencing embroidery, double-checking the position of the next design or section, as sometimes things change once the fabric is embroidered.

Self-adhesive tear-away stabilizer

1 Use paper scissors to cut a piece of self-adhesive tear-away stabilizer that is 1½in wider and longer than the hoop it is being used for. Hoop the stabilizer as you would fabric, with the protective coating uppermost in the hoop.

2 Use a pin or sharp object to score diagonal lines (piercing the protective coating only) that intersect through the center of the stabilizer in the hoop, as well as around the inside of the hoop. Then use a pin to lift each of the four sections of protective coating from the center (these should be removed easily with the aid of the score lines).

3 The design is then called up onto the screen. Make sure it is in the center of the screen and the needle is in the center of the design.

4 Place the hoop in the machine, then place the fabric to be embroidered over the sticky stabilizer in the hoop so the intersecting placement lines match those marked on the hoop and the needle sits over the intersection of the two lines. Also make sure that the top of the hoop marked on the fabric matches the top of the actual hoop once the fabric is placed on the stabilizer.

5 The idea of using sticky stabilizer in the hoop is so the fabric can be moved on the stabilizer rather than the design being moved on the screen, and to save re-hooping fabric time and time again. It also helps to achieve accurate placement with ease and precision.

6 It is recommended that a complete new piece of sticky stabilizer be used for each new embroidery, so that the fabric is held firm and stable, thus ensuring perfect embroidery results.

Embroidery

NOTE: Each 18in square block (finished size 15in square) of the Aquamarine Ambience *quilt can stand alone, so it can be made into a pillow, wall-hanging, tablecloth or runner. The colors can vary to suit your decor.*

1 It is recommended that your machine be serviced before you start this quilt, and that it is kept cleaned and oiled during the quilt's embroidery and construction.

2 Helmar's *Dust A Way* is great for keeping lint away from the bobbin and needle tension areas of your machine, by using compressed air.

3 All embroidery uses the Bernina Gold-Latch bobbin case (as the tension is or can be tightened when using a fine pre-wound bobbin; remove the cardboard from each side of the thread on the pre-wound bobbin before you insert it into the bobbin case so the bobbin monitor will work), Robison-Anton rayon embroidery thread in a Jeans 80 needle, the darning foot No 26, the basting stitch downloaded from the Bernina USA website and sticky stabilizer in the hoop.

4 A fine pre-wound bobbin is an essential ingredient to achieving perfect embroidery as the finer the bobbin thread the less bulk there is in any embroidery. A fine bobbin can reduce the embroidery bulk by up to one-third, ensuring flat smooth embroidery with little or no fabric puckering.

5 Robison-Anton rayon 40 embroidery threads ensure a shimmering and perfect embroidery result with a range of colors second to none on the market. The subtle change of thread colors that match the fabrics used in *Aquamarine Ambience* gives the embroidery a glistening effect as one color seems to run into another. As well, the nap silk fabrics and fabric circle inserts give the quilt the appearance of changing color, depending on where you're standing to look at it.

6 All embroidery is done from the center to the outside of each block, with designs being centred (in various measurements from the center of each block) over the marked vertical, horizontal and diagonal lines that intersect each block.

7 When positioning each embroidery design template, note the position that the design sits on the block alongside the previous embroidered design, and where the embroidery will overlap the inserted fabric circle.

8 Always refer to the picture of the block to check embroidery positions, and the direction the motif is facing on the block, and be careful not to embroider too close to (no closer than ½in) or over the marked 15in square that denotes the seam line of each block.

9 After each embroidery design is complete:

☼ clip the bobbin thread from the back of the basting stitch at intervals, then pull the needle thread from the top of the fabric to remove the basting stitch

☼ remove all excess stabilizer from the back of the block

☼ clip all jump threads and press the block.

You are now ready to set sail on the
Aquamarine Ambience sea,
on a Voyage that will take you
to creative shores.

Trooping the Colors

Aquamarine Ambience *uses two aqua/blue nap silk fabrics with threads that match and enhance these colors, thus reflecting the colors in the ocean. Should the colors used in* Aquamarine Ambience *not be those you are most comfortable working with (or perhaps they don't suit your needs), here are a few fabric and thread combinations (along with the pillows on page 96) to help you make an alternative color choice when you make this quilt.*

 A: Reds and blues

 B: Red and blue–green

Silk nap fabrics: blue napped with red and red napped with blue

Threads: Robison-Anton rayon 40 in Warm Wine (No 2496), TH Burgundy (No 2608), Candy Apple (No 2507) and Blue Ink (No 2440)

Silk nap fabrics: red napped with blue and green napped with blue

Threads: Robison-Anton rayon 40 in Warm Wine (No 2496), TH Burgundy (No 2608), Passion Rose (No 2499) and Green Forest (No 2451)

 ## C: Hot pink and red

Silk nap fabrics: red napped with hot pink and pink napped with red

Threads: Robison-Anton rayon 40 in Red Jubilee (No 2421), Cranberry (No 2270), Strawberry (No 2432) and Rosewood (No 2508)

 ## D: Peach and pink

Silk nap fabrics: pale apricot napped with orange and hot pink napped with yellow

Threads: Robison-Anton rayon 40 in Honeysuckle (No 2513), Shrimp (No 2246), Melonade (No 2512) and Mount Rose (No 2495)

 ## E: Lime green and cyclamen

Silk nap fabrics: lime green and hot pink and plain cyclamen silk

Threads: Robison-Anton rayon 40 in Desert Cactus (No 2544), Tamarack (No 2230), Sun Shadow (No 2548) and Strawberry (No 2432)

Finding your SeaLegs

Pillow Talk Pillow
Robyn Wilson and Jenny Haskins

To ensure we understood all the techniques used in the Aquamarine Ambience quilt, Rob and Jenny decided to have a little play with color and design using the same threads and fabrics Simon used in his quilt, but accenting the lime green thread and adding this fabric to the pillow.

Finished size of pillow: 17½in square

Materials

- Bernina Artista 730E embroidery machine and 255mm x 145mm hoop
- Bernina Artista Software V4 and transfer device
- Bernina Gold-Latch bobbin case to be used for embroidery
- *Aquamarine Ambience* design CD by Jenny Haskins (included with this book)
- 15in square of light green/blue nap silk dupione for frame (Color A)
- 12in square of dark green/blue nap silk dupione for circle (Color B)
- 6in x 45in strip of lime green nap silk
- 28in x 18in dark blue pillow cotton backing fabric
- 1yd lightweight fusible batting
- 14in square pillow insert
- Machine needle: Jeans 80
- Machine feet: darning foot No 26, patchwork ¼in foot No 37, open-toe appliqué foot No 20 and quilting guide, and the BSR (Bernina Stitch Regulator) foot No 42
- Threads: Robison-Anton rayon 40 embroidery threads: Bluestone (No 2515), Jungle Green (No 2597), Peapod (No 2456) and Green Forest (No 2451)
- Threads to match fabrics for construction, quilting and bobbins
- Pre-wound fine bobbins for embroidery, to reduce the bulk
- Self-adhesive tear-away stabilizer (must tear away easily and not be too sticky)
- *Cut A Round* tool (19in–6in) by Phillips Fiber Art
- 1 Clover chalk pencil in pink for marking the center square
- Rotary cutter (45mm), self-healing cutting mat and quilter's ruler
- Long fine glass-headed quilting pins
- Small thread clips to clip jump threads in embroidery
- Paper scissors to cut stabilizer
- Heavy-duty spray starch to stabilize the fabric
- Vellum tracing paper to print placement templates for embroidery designs
- Awl to punch holes in the placement templates
- Helmar's *Dust A Way* compressed air (to keep tension areas on the machine lint-free)
- General sewing requirements

Preparation

1   Go to the Bernina website (**www.berninausa.com**). Select *What's New*, then *FREE Downloads*, then *Free Embroidery Hoop Basting Designs*, then the appropriate hoop size to suit your machine. Now download this to your computer (*Aquamarine Ambience* designs use the 255mm x 145mm oval hoop). Follow the directions found on the website on how to use the basting stitch in conjunction with your embroidery designs.

2   Use the Artista design software and transfer device to transfer designs aa19 and aa31 to the computer; add basting stitch to each design and then transfer the designs to the machine and print templates for each design.

3   Go to pages 12-18 (in the instructions for the *Aquamarine Ambience* quilt) and read the directions for the following – Preparation, Embroidery, using the *Cut A Round* tool, vellum templates, tear-away self-adhesive (sticky) stabilizer, and *Jenny's Tricks of the Trade.*

4   Use the rotary cutter, self-healing cutting mat and quilter's ruler to cut from the:

Fusible batting:

☀ two, 15in squares to back the center of the pillow.

Pillow backing fabric:

☀ two, 14in x 18in rectangles to back the pillow.

Lime green nap silk and fusible batting:

☀ two, 2½in x 14in strips for the top and bottom of the pillow

☀ two, 2½in x 18in strips for the sides of the pillow.

Use a hot steam iron to fuse the batting to the back of the lime green silk strips.

5 Use the *Cut A Round* tool to cut from the:

Color A fabric:

☼ 9in hole in the center of the 15in square of silk (for a frame).

Color B fabric:

☼ 10in circle from the 12in square of silk for the circle insert.

Fusible batting:

☼ 9in circle to back the inserted fabric circle.

6 Refer to pages 14-15 for instructions on inserting the 10in fabric circle into the 9in circle in the 15in fabric frame. Press the seam to the center of the pillow and fuse the 9in circle of fusible batting to the back of the inserted circle, then the 15in square of batting to the back of the whole 15in square.

Quilting the center circle

7 Use the open-toe appliqué foot No 20 and quilting guide, Bluestone (No 2515) rayon 40 embroidery thread in the Jeans 80 needle, a pre-wound bobbin and a straight stitch to quilt a ⅝in diagonal grid in the center circle only (of the 15in silk square), starting and stopping at the edge of the inserted fabric circle that is backed with fusible batting.

Stitch-building

8 Use the open-toe appliqué foot No 20, Jungle Green (No 2597) rayon 40 embroidery thread in a Jeans 80 needle, and a pre-wound bobbin in the gold-latch bobbin case to sew stitch 117, width 6, pattern extend 2 around the center fabric circle, centered over the seam line.

9 Use Green Forest (No 2451) rayon 40 embroidery thread to sew stitch 133, width 6, length 3.5, centered over stitch 117.

Embroidery

10 Use the (sticky) self-adhesive tear-away stabilizer in the hoop, a pre-wound bobbin in the gold-latch bobbin case, rayon 40 embroidery thread in the Jeans 80 needle and the darning foot No 26 for all embroidery.

11 Make sure you have the basting stitch around your two embroidery designs before transferring them to the sewing machine.

12 Center the vellum template for design aa19 over the center of the pillow front, making sure the leaves sit on both sides of both the vertical and horizontal divide lines on each side of the center of the fabric.

13 Place the hoop in the machine, center the needle over the design, and place the fabric over the stabilizer (matching vertical and horizontal lines on the fabric with those marked on the hoop). Stitch the basting stitch first, then the embroidery design in the following sequence:

☼ color 1 leaves – Green Forest (No 2451)

☼ color 2 center flower – Jungle Green (No 2597)

☼ color 3 flower center – Peapod (No 2456)

☼ colors 4 and 5 – DO NOT STITCH.

14 Remove the basting stitch and then the fabric from the hoop and press your work.

15 Position the vellum template for design aa31 in each corner of the 15in square over the diagonal lines, using the photo as a guide Then repeat step 13 to sew design aa31 in each corner of the 15in square in the following sequence:

☼ color 1 top center outline leaves – Peapod (No 2456)

☼ color 2 side circles – Jungle Green (No 2597)

☼ color 3 center of circles – Bluestone (No 2515)

☼ color 4 bottom center leaves – Green Forest (No 2451)

☼ color 5 three small flowers – Peapod (No 2456)

☼ color 6 side leaves – Green Forest (No 2451)

Repeat step 14.

16 Fuse a second 15in square of batting to the back of the 15in embroidered square for the center of the pillow, then square it up to 14in.

Attaching the borders and free-motion quilting

17 Use the patchwork ¼in foot No 37, construction thread in the Jeans 80 needle and bobbin (in the normal bobbin case) and a straight stitch to attach the borders to the pillow.

18 Attach the two, 2½in x 14in green silk strips backed with fusible batting to the top and bottom of the embroidered 14in square. Press the seams to the outside edge of the pillow, then trim the ends of the strips in line with the center square.

19 Attach the two, 2½in x 18in green silk strips backed with fusible batting to the sides of the embroidered 14in square. Press the seams to the outside edge of the pillow, then trim the ends of the strips in line with the sides of the top and bottom border strips.

20 Use the BSR foot No 42, a pre-wound bobbin in the gold-latch bobbin case, the Jeans 80 needle threaded with Peapod (No 2456) and a straight stitch to freehand-stipple-quilt around the embroidery designs on the center square of the pillow, extending into the lime green pillow borders.

Construction

21 Turn under a double ½in hem on the 18in side of one end of each of the two, 14in x 18in rectangles of fabric to back the pillow, then stitch it down.

22 Overlap these two pieces, so the top piece has the wrong side of fabric to the right side of the underneath fabric, with hemmed edges facing the outside edge of the pillow, until the overlapped fabric pieces form an 18in square. Pin down the overlaps along the raw fabric edges, then stitch them together with a narrow hem along the raw fabric overlap edge only.

23 Place the overlapped pillow backing over the pillow front, right sides together, and pin around the edges. Use the patchwork ¼in foot No 37 and construction thread to sew around the four sides of the pillow.

24 Turn the pillow to the right side, making sure the corners are pushed out, and press both the pillow front and back.

25 Use Jungle Green (No 2597) in the needle and thread that matches the backing fabric in the bobbin to stitch-in-the-ditch through both the pillow top and the backing in the seam line around the center pillow square (where the lime green borders are attached to the pillow front).

26 Place the 14in insert in the pillow.

How easy was that?
Now that you have your 'sea legs', you are ready to start your Aquamarine Ambience quilt voyage with confidence, excitement and great enthusiasm!

Turn to the back of the book for *From the Captain's Table*, a table runner, as well as *From the Captain's Galley, Bunk* and *From the Captain's Galley*, two more pillows you may also like to try. These are in different color stories, and Rob and Jen had a lot of fun making them after learning these techniques. The table runner is a great way to use up the circles cut from the center of the frame fabric used for Simon's *Aquamarine Ambience* quilt.

Aquamarine Ambience

Simon's Aquamarine Ambience *quilt* has been designed as a whole quilt with the colors and fabrics reflecting those of the changing colors in the crystal clear waters found on the coastline of Australia. He has used embroidery designs found on the accompanying CD.

The quilt is easy to stitch and embroider, and not only is it achievable by a novice, it is also challenging enough for the more experienced artist, inspiring as well as building confidence in all who choose to take up the challenge.

The techniques and embroidery designs used in *Aquamarine Ambience* can be used on pillows (see pages 98 and 102), table runners or cloths (see page 88), as well as on clothing and a variety of home decor items.

So take to the seas of *Aquamarine Ambience*, sail forth on the sparkling waters of color and design, and experience the exhilaration that pure creativity and achievement bring on this voyage of creative discovery!

NOTE: *In keeping with quilting traditions, imperial measurements are used throughout the directions for the Aquamarine Ambience quilt.*

Finished size of quilt: 67½in x 85in
Finished size of each block: 15in square
Finished size of sashing: 2½in wide
Finished size of borders: 6¾in wide

Provisions for the Voyage

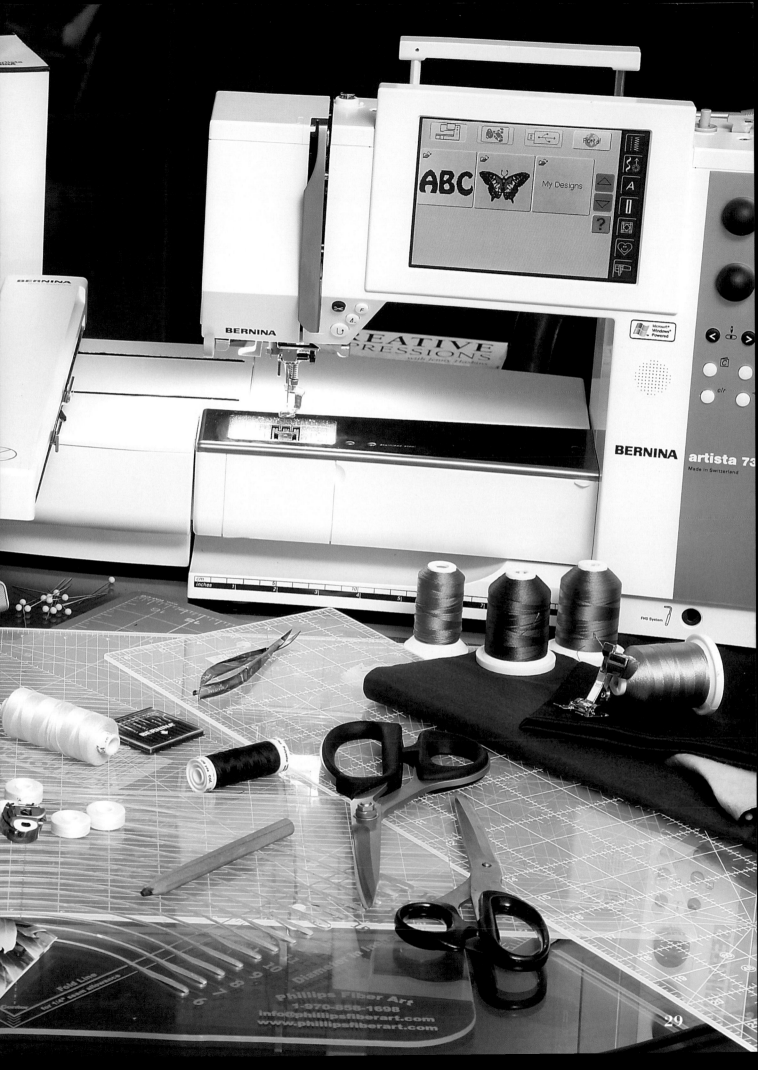

Aquamarine Ambience
Quilt

Materials

- Bernina Artista 730E embroidery machine and 255mm x 145mm hoop
- Bernina Artista Software V4 and transfer device
- Bernina Gold-Latch bobbin case to be used for embroidery
- *Aquamarine Ambience* design CD by Jenny Haskins (included with this book)
- 4½yd x 45in light green/blue nap silk dupione for circles, sashing and binding (Color A)
- 6yd x 45in dark green/blue nap silk dupione for blocks and borders (Color B)
- 6½yd x 45in dark blue cotton backing fabric (less if you do not wish to have the join centered)
- 7yd x 36in lightweight fusible batting
- Machine needle: Jeans 80
- Machine feet: darning foot No 26, patchwork ¼in foot No 37 and construction foot No 1
- Threads: Robison-Anton rayon 40 embroidery threads: 6 spools Bluestone (No 2515), 4 spools Jungle Green (No 2597), 2 spools Peapod (No 2456) and 1 spool Green Forest (No 2451)

- Threads to match fabrics for construction, quilting and bobbins
- Pre-wound fine bobbins for embroidery, to reduce the bulk
- Self-adhesive tear-away stabilizer (must tear away easily and not be too sticky)
- *Cut A Round* tool (19in–6in) by Phillips Fiber Art
- 4 Clover chalk pencils in pink
- Rotary cutter (45mm), self-healing cutting mat and quilter's ruler
- 15½in quilter's square
- Long fine glass-headed quilting pins
- Small thread clips
- Paper scissors to cut stabilizer
- Heavy-duty spray starch
- Vellum tracing paper to print placement templates
- Awl to punch holes in the placement templates
- Helmar's *Dust A Way* compressed air (to keep tension areas on the machine lint-free)
- Sticky tape
- Hand-sewing needle
- General sewing requirements

Block 1

This is the start of your trip,
where you lose sight
of the shore and set sail
with confidence – bon voyage!

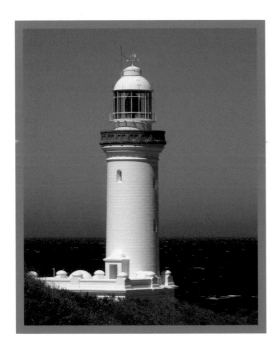

*The embroidery designs are done
on an 18in square block with a fabric
circle insert. The designs are centered
over the vertical, horizontal and diagonal
lines marked on the block, using the
photo and vellum templates as a guide
for accurate embroidery placement.
Embroidery designs are done in the
following sequence, with a new piece of
stabilizer for each.*

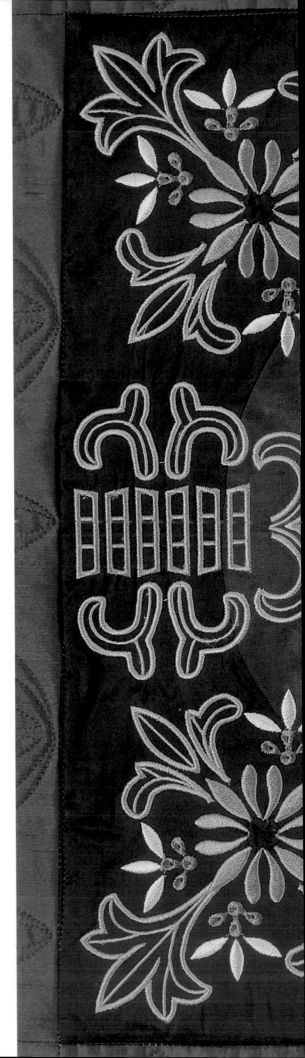

33

Block 1

aa01

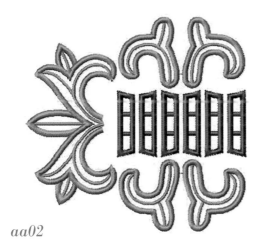

aa02

aa03

1   Center: design aa01 (no template printed) centered on the block so the 'arms' of the design are centered on the vertical and horizontal lines and the 'circles' are centered on the diagonal lines.

☀ Color 1 – Peapod (No 2456)
☀ Color 2 – Bluestone (No 2515)
☀ Color 3 – Jungle Green (No 2597)
☀ Color 4 – Peapod (No 2456)

2   Vertical and horizontal lines: design aa02 (print one template) centered over these lines so the designs are vertical.

☀ Color 1 – Bluestone (No 2515)
☀ Color 2 – Jungle Green (No 2597)
☀ Color 3 – Bluestone (No 2515)

3   Diagonal lines in each corner of the block: design aa03 (print one template) centered over these lines so the designs are vertical.

☀ Color 1 – Bluestone (No 2515)
☀ Color 2 – Jungle Green (No 2597)
☀ Color 3 – Bluestone (No 2515)
☀ Color 4 – Peapod (No 2456)
☀ Color 5 – Green Forest (No 2451)

aa02

aa03

aa03

aa02

aa02

aa01

aa03

aa02

aa03

Block 2

*The embroidery designs are done
on an 18in square block with a fabric
circle insert. The designs are centered
over the vertical, horizontal and diagonal
lines marked on the block, using the
photo and vellum templates as a guide
for accurate embroidery placement.
Embroidery designs are done in the
following sequence, with a new piece of
stabilizer for each.*

37

aa04

Block 2

1   Center: design aa04 (no template printed) centered in the block.

☼ Color 1 – Bluestone (No 2515)

☼ Color 2 – Peapod (No 2456)

2   Vertical and horizontal lines: design aa05 (four templates printed). Refer to the photo as a guide to combine these templates, making sure the designs touch at the bottom and are straight both vertically and horizontally. Hold them together with sticky tape.

Center the combination template over the block so each design is centered over either a vertical or horizontal line on each side of the center of the block, to mark the individual embroidery placement positions. Mark the positions for all four designs (the designs are vertical on each line) from the combination template, embroidering the first and second designs opposite, then use a single template to mark the placement position for the next two designs, ensuring the third and fourth embroidery designs connect with the first and second in the correct manner.

☼ Color 1 – Jungle Green (No 2597)

☼ Color 2 – Bluestone (No 2515)

☼ Color 3 – Peapod (No 2456)

☼ Color 4 – Peapod (No 2456)

☼ Color 5 – Green Forest (No 2451)

aa05

3   Diagonal lines: design aa06 (print one template) centered over these lines in each corner of the block.

☼ Color 1 – Bluestone (No 2515)

☼ Color 2 – Jungle Green (No 2597)

☼ Color 3 – Peapod (No 2456)

aa06

4   Vertical and horizontal lines: design aa07 (print one template; this is positioned so a flower sits on each side of the center three embroidered leaves) centered over these lines at the top of the Step 2 aa05 embroidery.

☼ Color 1 – Jungle Green (No 2597)

☼ Color 2 – Peapod (No 2456)

aa07

aa07

aa05

aa06

aa06

aa07

aa05

aa05

aa07

aa04

aa06

aa06

aa05

aa07

Block 3

*The embroidery designs are done
on an 18in square block with a fabric
circle insert. The designs are centered
over the vertical, horizontal and diagonal
lines marked on the block, using the
photo and vellum templates as a guide
for accurate embroidery placement.
Embroidery designs are done in the
following sequence, with a new piece of
stabilizer for each.*

41

Block 3

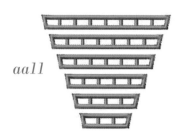

aa08   *aa11*

aa09

aa10

1   Center: design aa08 (no template printed) centered so the design is vertical on the block.

☼ Color 1 – Jungle Green (No 2597)

☼ Color 2 – Green Forest (No 2451)

2   Center: design aa09 (no template printed).
To embroider aa09, rotate the block 90 degrees clockwise from the position it was under the needle for embroidery design aa08. Design aa09 should now stitch centered vertically in the block.

☼ Color 1 – Jungle Green (No 2597)

☼ Color 2 – Green Forest (No 2451)

☼ Color 3 – Bluestone (No 2515)

☼ Color 4 – Peapod (No 2456)

☼ Color 5 – Green Forest (No 2451)

☼ Color 6 – Peapod (No 2456)

☼ Color 7 – Bluestone (No 2515)

3   Diagonal lines: design aa10 (print one template) centered vertically over these lines in each corner of the block.

These corner designs actually touch the points of the center design aa09 and come very close to the 15in marked square on the block. Very accurate placement of this design is necessary to ensure there is no embroidery 'outside the marked square'.

☼ Color 1 – Peapod (No 2456)

☼ Color 2 – Bluestone (No 2515)

☼ Color 3 – Jungle Green (No 2597)

☼ Color 4 – Green Forest (No 2451)

☼ Color 5 – Jungle Green (No 2597)

☼ Color 6 – Peapod (No 2456)

☼ Color 7 – Bluestone (No 2515)

4   Vertical and horizontal lines: design aa11 (print one template).

When marking the placement position for this design, note the direction of the design (when embroidering the design, the fabric should be placed over the stabilizer under the needle so the bulk of the fabric is to the front of the hoop); the second bar from the bottom of the design should sit inside the fabric circle insert.

☼ Color 1 – Bluestone (No 2515)

aa11

aa08

aa10

aa10

aa11

aa09

aa11

aa10

aa10

aa11

Block 4

Congratulations!
You are now one-quarter of the way
through your block voyage.

*The embroidery designs are done
on an 18in square block with a fabric
circle insert. The designs are centered
over the vertical, horizontal and diagonal
lines marked on the block, using the
photo and vellum templates as a guide
for accurate embroidery placement.
Embroidery designs are done in the
following sequence, with a new piece of
stabilizer for each.*

45

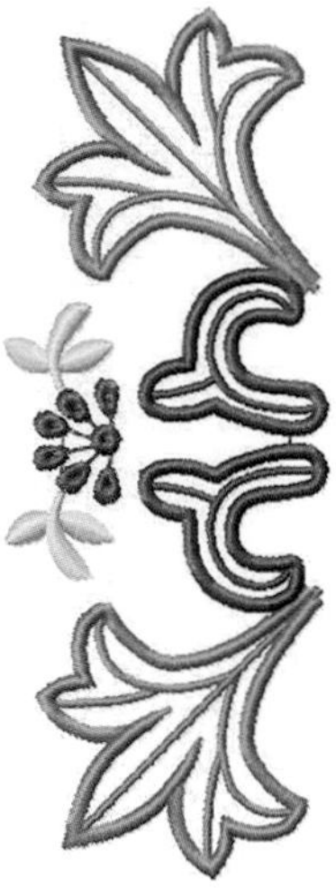

aa12

aa13

aa14

aa15

Block 4

1 Center: combination design aa12 and aa13 (print one template for each design). Combine the templates so they make one design (using the photo as a guide), then hold them together with sticky tape. This combination design is centered in the block; the pointed designs are centered over the diagonal lines and the curved designs sit on either side of the vertical and horizontal lines on each side of the center of the block. Mark the placement positions for both designs.

(a) Design aa12 is embroidered first, stitching vertically as follows:

☼ Color 1 – Bluestone (No 2515)
☼ Color 2 – Jungle Green (No 2597)
☼ Color 3 – Peapod (No 2456)
☼ Color 4 – Green Forest (No 2451)

(b) Design aa13: replace the combination template for both designs so that design aa12 on the template sits over the embroidered aa12 in order to check the placement position for aa13, which is embroidered second, stitching vertically as follows:

☼ Color 1 – Bluestone (No 2515)
☼ Color 2 – Jungle Green (No 2597)
☼ Color 3 – Peapod (No 2456)
☼ Color 4 – Green Forest (No 2451)
☼ Color 5 – Bluestone (No 2515)
☼ Color 6 – Peapod (No 2456)

2 Vertical and horizontal lines: design aa14 (print one template) centered over these lines.

☼ Color 1 – Bluestone (No 2515)
☼ Color 2 – Peapod (No 2456)
☼ Color 3 – Peapod (No 2456)
☼ Color 4 – Green Forest (No 2451)
☼ Color 5 – Peapod (No 2456)
☼ Color 6 – Green Forest (No 2451)
☼ Color 7 – Jungle Green (No 2597)
☼ Color 8 – Peapod (No 2456)

3 Diagonal lines: design aa15 (print one template) centered over these lines so the design is vertical.

☼ Color 1 – Bluestone (No 2515)
☼ Color 2 – Jungle Green (No 2597)
☼ Color 3 – Bluestone (No 2515)
☼ Color 4 – Green Forest (No 2451)
☼ Color 5 – Peapod (No 2456)
☼ Color 6 – Peapod (No 2456)
☼ Color 7 – Green Forest (No 2451)
☼ Color 8 – Peapod (No 2456)
☼ Color 9 – Green Forest (No 2451)
☼ Color 10 – Green Forest (No 2451)

Block 5

*The embroidery designs are done
on an 18in square block with a fabric
circle insert. The designs are centered
over the vertical, horizontal and diagonal
lines marked on the block, using the
photo and vellum templates as a guide
for accurate embroidery placement.
Embroidery designs are done in the
following sequence, with a new piece of
stabilizer for each.*

49

aa16

aa17

aa18

Block 5

1 Center: design aa16 (no template printed) centered in the block so a leaf spray sits on either side of all eight divide lines.
- ☼ Color 1 – Bluestone (No 2515)
- ☼ Color 2 – Jungle Green (No 2597)
- ☼ Color 3 – Peapod (No 2456)

2 Diagonal lines: design aa17 (print one template) centered vertically over these lines in the corners of the block.

NOTE: The points of the design just overlap the inserted fabric circle in the center of the block. Be very accurate with the placement of this design and make sure it clears the 15in marked lines.

- ☼ Color 1 – Bluestone (No 2515)
- ☼ Color 2 – Peapod (No 2456)
- ☼ Color 3 – Green Forest (No 2451)
- ☼ Color 4 – Jungle Green (No 2597)
- ☼ Color 5 – Peapod (No 2456)

3 Vertical and horizontal lines: design aa18 (print one template) centered horizontally over these lines.
- ☼ Color 1 – Jungle Green (No 2597)
- ☼ Color 2 – Bluestone (No 2515)
- ☼ Color 3 – Peapod (No 2456)
- ☼ Color 4 – Green Forest (No 2451)
- ☼ Color 5 – Jungle Green (No 2597)
- ☼ Color 6 – Peapod (No 2456)

Block 6

*The embroidery designs are done
on an 18in square block with a fabric
circle insert. The designs are centered
over the vertical, horizontal and diagonal
lines marked on the block, using the
photo and vellum templates as a guide
for accurate embroidery placement.
Embroidery designs are done in the
following sequence, with a new piece of
stabilizer for each.*

53

Block 6

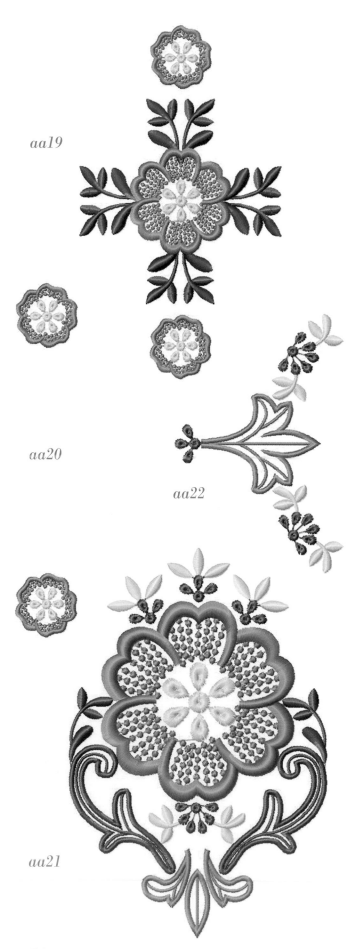

aa19

aa20

aa22

aa21

1   Center: design aa19 (no template printed) centered so a leaf spray sits on each side of the vertical and horizontal lines and a flower is centered above the leaves on the vertical line on the block.

☀ Color 1 – Jungle Green (No 2597)

☀ Color 2 – Bluestone (No 2515)

☀ Color 3 – Peapod (No 2456)

☀ Color 4 – Bluestone (No 2515)

☀ Color 5 – Peapod (No 2456)

2   Center: design aa20 (no template printed). To embroider aa20, rotate the block 90 degrees clockwise from the position it was under the needle for embroidery design aa19. Design aa20 should now be centered vertically in the block.

☀ Color 1 – Bluestone (No 2515)

☀ Color 2 – Peapod (No 2456)

3   Diagonal lines: design aa21 (print one template) centered vertically over these lines in the corners of the block.

☀ Color 1 – Bluestone (No 2515)

☀ Color 2 – Jungle Green (No 2597)

☀ Color 3 – Peapod (No 2456)

☀ Color 4 – Green Forest (No 2451)

4   Vertical and horizontal lines: design aa22 (print one template) centered vertically over these lines.

☀ Color 1 – Bluestone (No 2515)

☀ Color 2 – Green Forest (No 2451)

☀ Color 3 – Peapod (No 2456)

☀ Color 4 – Green Forest (No 2451)

aa22

aa21

aa21

aa22

aa20

aa19

aa22

aa21

aa21

aa22

Block 7

Congratulations!
You are now halfway through
your block voyage, and enjoying
smooth sailing, we hope!

*The embroidery designs are done
on an 18in square block with a fabric
circle insert. The designs are centered
over the vertical, horizontal and diagonal
lines marked on the block, using the
photo and vellum templates as a guide
for accurate embroidery placement.
Embroidery designs are done in the
following sequence, with a new piece of
stabilizer for each.*

aa23

aa24

aa25

Block 7

1   Center: design aa23 (print four templates).
Refer to the photo to combine the four templates,
so each design just touches on each side with the
connecting design, to form one design.
Hold them together with sticky tape. Centre the
combination template over the block so each
design is centered over either a vertical or a
horizontal line, on each side of the center of the
block, to mark the individual embroidery
placement positions for design aa23. Mark the
positions for all four designs from the
combination template, embroidering the first
and second designs opposite, then use a single
template to mark placement positions for the
next two designs, ensuring the third and fourth
embroidery designs connect with the first and
second in the correct manner.

☀ Color 1 – Bluestone (No 2515)

☀ Color 2 – Jungle Green (No 2597)

☀ Color 3 – Peapod (No 2456)

2   Diagonal lines: design aa24 (print one
template) centered vertically over these lines
in each corner of the block.

☀ Color 1 – Bluestone (No 2515)

☀ Color 2 – Jungle Green (No 2597)

☀ Color 3 – Peapod (No 2456)

3   Vertical and horizontal lines: design aa25
(print one template) centered horizontally over
these lines.

☀ Color 1 – Bluestone (No 2515)

☀ Color 2 – Peapod (No 2456)

☀ Color 3 – Peapod (No 2456)

☀ Color 4 – Green Forest (No 2451)

☀ Color 5 – Green Forest (No 2451)

☀ Color 6 – Bluestone (No 2515)

aa24

aa25

aa24

aa23

aa23

aa25

aa23

aa25

aa23

aa23

aa24

aa24

aa25

Block 8

*The embroidery designs are done
on an 18in square block with a fabric
circle insert. The designs are centered
over the vertical, horizontal and diagonal
lines marked on the block, using the
photo and vellum templates as a guide
for accurate embroidery placement.
Embroidery designs are done in the
following sequence, with a new piece of
stabilizer for each.*

61

aa26

Block 8

1   Center: design aa26 (no template printed) centered in the block so a leaf spray sits on a vertical or horizontal line on each side of the center of the block and the flowers are centered over the diagonal lines.

☀ Color 1 – Bluestone (No 2515)
☀ Color 2 – Peapod (No 2456)
☀ Color 3 – Jungle Green (No 2597)
☀ Color 4 – Peapod (No 2456)
☀ Color 5 – Green Forest (No 2451)

2   Diagonal lines: design aa27 (print one template) centered horizontally over these lines in the corners of the block.

☀ Color 1 – Bluestone (No 2515)
☀ Color 2 – Jungle Green (No 2597)
☀ Color 3 – Bluestone (No 2515)
☀ Color 4 – Peapod (No 2456)
☀ Color 5 – Jungle Green (No 2597)
☀ Color 6 – Peapod (No 2456)
☀ Color 7 – Green Forest (No 2451)

3   Vertical and horizontal lines: design aa28 (print one template) centered vertically over these lines.

☀ Color 1 – Bluestone (No 2515)
☀ Color 2 – Peapod (No 2456)
☀ Color 3 – Jungle Green (No 2597)

aa27

aa28

aa27

aa28

aa27

aa28

aa28

aa26

aa28

aa27

aa27

aa28

Block 9

*The embroidery designs are done
on an 18in square block with a fabric
circle insert. The designs are centered
over the vertical, horizontal and diagonal
lines marked on the block, using the
photo and vellum templates as a guide
for accurate embroidery placement.
Embroidery designs are done in the
following sequence, with a new piece of
stabilizer for each.*

Block 9

aa29

1   Center: design aa29 (no template printed) centered over the block so the center leaf of the corner designs is centered on the diagonal lines.

☼ Color 1 – Bluestone (No 2515)
☼ Color 2 – Jungle Green (No 2597)
☼ Color 3 – Peapod (No 2456)
☼ Color 4 – Peapod (No 2456)
☼ Color 5 – Green Forest (No 2451)

2   Vertical and horizontal lines: design aa30 (print one template) centered over these lines on the horizontal so the bottom curve of the design follows that of the inserted fabric circle and the three leaves sit just below it.

☼ Color 1 – Bluestone (No 2515)
☼ Color 2 – Jungle Green (No 2597)
☼ Color 3 – Peapod (No 2456)
☼ Color 4 – Peapod (No 2456)
☼ Color 5 – Green Forest (No 2451)
☼ Color 6 – Bluestone (No 2515)

aa30

3   Diagonal lines: design aa31 (print one template) centered horizontally over these lines in the corner of each block.

☼ Color 1 – Bluestone (No 2515)
☼ Color 2 – Bluestone (No 2515)
☼ Color 3 – Peapod (No 2456)
☼ Color 4 – Peapod (No 2456)
☼ Color 5 – Green Forest (No 2451)
☼ Color 6 – Jungle Green (No 2597)

aa31

aa31

aa31

aa30

aa30

aa29

aa30

aa31

aa30

aa31

Block 10

Congratulations!
You are now three-quarters
of the way through your block journey.
The end of the voyage is in sight!

*The embroidery designs are done
on an 18in square block with a fabric
circle insert. The designs are centered
over the vertical, horizontal and diagonal
lines marked on the block, using the
photo and vellum templates as a guide
for accurate embroidery placement.
Embroidery designs are done in the
following sequence, with a new piece of
stabilizer for each.*

Block 10

1   Center: design aa32 (no template printed) centered in the block.

☀ Color 1 – Peapod (No 2456)

☀ Color 2 – Jungle Green (No 2597)

2   Horizontal line: design aa33 (print one template) centered vertically over this line on each side of the center of the block so the leaf sprays just touch the inside edge of the inserted fabric circle and the flower is centered over the horizontal line.

☀ Color 1 – Green Forest (No 2451)

☀ Color 2 – Jungle Green (No 2597)

☀ Color 3 – Bluestone (No 2515)

☀ Color 4 – Peapod (No 2456)

☀ Color 5 – Bluestone (No 2515)

☀ Color 6 – Peapod (No 2456)

☀ Color 7 – Peapod (No 2456)

☀ Color 8 – Green Forest (No 2451)

3   Vertical line: design aa34 (print one template) centered horizontally over this line on each side of the center of the block so the leaf sprays just touch the inside edge of the inserted fabric circle and the flower is centered over the vertical line.

☀ Color 1 – Green Forest (No 2451)

☀ Color 2 – Jungle Green (No 2597)

☀ Color 3 – Bluestone (No 2515)

☀ Color 4 – Peapod (No 2456)

☀ Color 5 – Peapod (No 2456)

☀ Color 6 – Green Forest (No 2451)

4   Vertical and horizontal lines: design aa35 (print one template) centered horizontally over these lines above design aa34 so the leaf sprays touch and match.

☀ Color 1 – Bluestone (No 2515)

☀ Color 2 – Peapod (No 2456)

☀ Color 3 – Green Forest (No 2451)

☀ Color 4 – Jungle Green (No 2597)

5   Diagonal lines: design aa36 (print one template) centered over these lines in each corner of the block.

☀ Color 1 – Bluestone (No 2515)

aa32

aa36

aa33

aa34

aa35

Block 11

Land is in sight.
Off-shore winds, seagulls and the
promise of an amazing journey's end
make you forget any hardships!

*The embroidery designs are done
on an 18in square block with a fabric
circle insert. The designs are centered
over the vertical, horizontal and diagonal
lines marked on the block, using the
photo and vellum templates as a guide
for accurate embroidery placement.
Embroidery designs are done in the
following sequence, with a new piece of
stabilizer for each.*

73

aa37

Block 11

aa38

1   Center: design aa37 (no template printed) centered in the block.

☀ Color 1 – Bluestone (No 2515)

☀ Color 2 – Peapod (No 2456)

2   Diagonal lines: design aa38 (print one template) centered vertically over these lines in the corners of the block.

☀ Color 1 – Bluestone (No 2515)

☀ Color 2 – Jungle Green (No 2597)

☀ Color 3 – Peapod (No 2456)

☀ Color 4 – Peapod (No 2456)

☀ Color 5 – Green Forest (No 2451)

3   Vertical and horizontal lines: design aa39 (print one template) centered vertically on these lines so the center of the bars is centered with the point on the center leaf on the leaf sprays from design aa38.

☀ Color 1 – Bluestone (No 2515)

☀ Color 2 – Peapod (No 2456)

☀ Color 3 – Green Forest (No 2451)

☀ Color 4 – Jungle Green (No 2597)

aa39

aa39

aa38

aa38

aa39

aa39

aa38

aa37

aa38

aa39

Block 12

*The embroidery designs are done
on an 18in square block with a fabric
circle insert. The designs are centered
over the vertical, horizontal and diagonal
lines marked on the block, using the
photo and vellum templates as a guide
for accurate embroidery placement.
Embroidery designs are done in the
following sequence, with a new piece of
stabilizer for each.*

aa40

aa41

Block 12

1 Center: design aa40 (no template printed) centered in the block.

☀ Color 1 - Bluestone (No 2515)

☀ Color 2 - Peapod (No 2456)

2 Diagonal lines: design aa41 (print one template) centered vertically on these lines in each corner of the block so the side leaves just connect on each side of the design around the embroidered flower in the center of the block.

☀ Color 1 - Jungle Green (No 2597)

☀ Color 2 - Bluestone (No 2515)

☀ Color 3 - Peapod (No 2456)

☀ Color 4 - Green Forest (No 2451)

3 Vertical and horizontal lines: design aa42 (print one template) centered vertically on these lines so the fourth bar down from the narrow top just sits on the edge of the inserted fabric circle.

☀ Color 1 - Bluestone (No 2515)

☀ Color 2 - Peapod (No 2456)

☀ Color 3 - Green Forest (No 2451)

The gang plank is down,
streamers fill the air you and are
preparing to disembark.
Congratulations!
You have finished the 12 blocks!

aa42

aa41

aa42

aa41

aa42

aa42

aa40

aa41

aa42

aa41

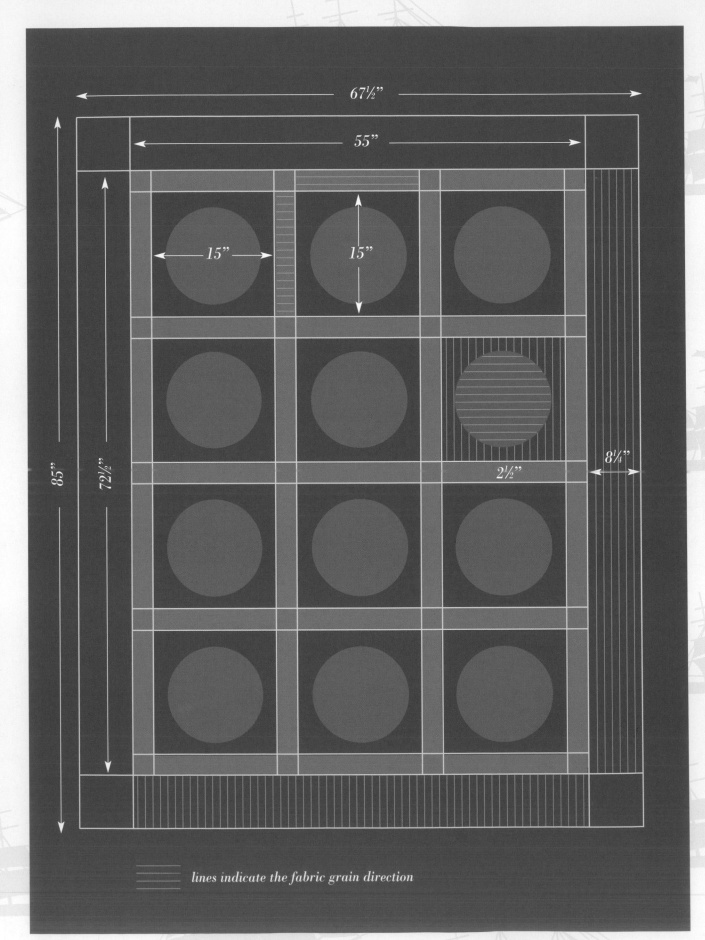

lines indicate the fabric grain direction

Reading the Map
Putting it together

Squaring up the blocks

1 Make sure that all excess stabilizer is removed from the back of each block, all jump threads are clipped, and the blocks are pressed flat and true to grain.

2 Center the 15½in quilter's square over each block on the self-healing cutting mat, matching the vertical and horizontal lines on the square ruler with those marked on the block to maintain the center of the block and embroidery, then cut around the square using the rotary cutter to square up each block.

3 Lay the blocks out in rows on a large flat surface, such as a cleared and clean carpeted floor, and refer to the flat picture of the quilt with the blocks numbered (see page 33).

4 Mark the top of each block with a small label, ensuring the nap grain of the block frame fabric runs vertically, and the nap grain in the fabric circles runs horizontally. Number each block and then put the blocks in four piles – one for each block row – with the lowest number for that row on the top.

Cutting the sashing and border strips

NOTE: We are cutting nap fabric, so to keep the grain running the same way for the whole quilt it is important to note when to cut with the grain and when to cut against it, in order to achieve a consistency of color for the whole quilt. The nap grain direction established for the blocks for each fabric will continue when cutting the sashing and border fabric strips. Again, allow yourself uninterrupted time, take your time, measure twice and cut once to avoid disappointment.

5 Use the rotary cutter, self-healing cutting mat and quilter's ruler to cut from:

Color A fabric and fusible batting

☼ 16, 3in x 15in strips against the grain of the fabric for the vertical sashing strips

☼ 15, 3in x 15in strips with the grain of the fabric for the horizontal sashing strips

☼ 20, 3in squares to join the sashing strips.

Color B fabric and fusible batting

☼ two, 6½in x 73in strips with the grain of the fabric for the side borders

☼ two, 6½in x 55½in strips against the grain of the fabric for the top and bottom border strips

☼ four, 6½in squares to join the borders.

6 Use a hot steam iron to fuse the batting to the back of each matching fabric piece, making sure you label the top of each strip and its position in the quilt. The squares can be turned to suit the fabric strips to which they are being joined.

Joining the blocks into rows with sashing strips

JENNY'S TIP: You will need to have your wits about you when joining the sashing and borders to the blocks to ensure the nap runs in the right direction throughout the quilt. Make sure your time will be uninterrupted and that you are not tired.

7 All construction uses construction thread in the Jeans 80 needle and bobbin (using the normal bobbin case), with the patchwork ¼in foot No 37 and a straight stitch.

Sashing strips are cut from Color A fabric

8 Lay the blocks out in sequence (both block and row) with the blocks the right way up, the marked top of the block to the top of the quilt and all consistent, then lay the vertical sashing strips between the blocks, ensuring the nap in the fabric is all going in the one direction (the fabric in the sashing strips is cut against the grain).

9 Join the blocks into rows (starting and finishing each row with a vertical sashing strip) in the following sequence:

JENNY'S TIP: Mark the top of each block row (each block is symmetrical and thus top and bottom of block rows are the same) to ensure the rows are joined together with the nap of the fabric running consistently in each row.

Row 1
☼ blocks 1, 2 and 3: Label block row 1
Row 2
☼ blocks 4, 5 and 6: Label block row 2
Row 3
☼ blocks 7, 8 and 9: Label block row 3
Row 4
☼ blocks 10, 11 and 12: Label block row 4

10 Press all the seams open from the back of the batting using a hot steam iron.

11 Join three 15½in horizontal sashing strips (cut with the fabric grain) together with the four 3in squares, starting and finishing with a square, to make a 55½in length. Make sure the fabric grain of the squares matches that of the sashing. Join five lengths in this way.

12 Press all the seams open.

Putting it together

JENNY'S TIP: Again, lay the rows of blocks out on a large flat surface, making sure each row has the nap fabrics running in the right direction, and that the top of each row is at the top of the block. (Remember, all the embroidered blocks are symmetrical, so careful attention needs to be given to the consistency of the nap direction in order to avoid disappointment.)

13 In the following sequence, join the block rows together with the 55½in sashing strips, matching the 3in square seams with those of the vertical sashing strips:

☼ horizontal sashing strip to each side of block rows 1 and 4; press the seams open

☼ horizontal sashing strip to join block rows 2 and 3 together; press the seams open

☼ join block rows 1, 2 and 3 together by stitching the lower sashing of block row 1 to the top of block row 2; press the seam open

☼ join all the block rows together by stitching the bottom of block row 3 to the top edge of the sashing at the top of block row 4; press the seam open.

14 Press the quilt from the front of the fabric, labelling the top of the quilt.

Quilt borders are cut from Color B fabric

15 Join a 6½in x 55½in border strip (cut against the grain) to the top and bottom of the quilt.

16 Join a 6½in square to each end of the two 73in border strips, matching the fabric grain of the squares to that of the border strips, thus extending the side border strips to 85in; press the seams open.

17 Join the 85in border strips to each side of the quilt, matching the seams of the squares with those of the top and bottom border strips; press the seams open.

18 Use a spray bottle and clean water to mist the quilt; this removes the chalk pencil lines and markings. A clean cloth may be used to gently rub persistent lines in order to remove all chalk pencil markings from the quilt.

Quilting

19 Cut the 6½yd backing fabric into two 3¼yd lengths, then join them down the center to make a 3½yd x 90in rectangle to back the quilt.

20 *Aquamarine Ambience* was quilted by Joanne Knott. She used a computerised long-arm sewing machine and designs chosen by Simon. All seams are stitched in the ditch with the sashing and borders elaborately quilted. As the embroidery designs are so intense on each block, no quilting was done on the embroidered blocks. You may choose to do some outline quilting on some of the embroidery designs if you think the blocks need to be held to the backing fabric.

21 You may choose to quilt your quilt in a way that best suits your skills, time and pocket, but remember that Bernina now has its magic BSR (Bernina Stitch Regulator) foot, which has a built-in stitch length regulator that makes it easy to achieve perfect freehand quilting.

Binding

22 From the Color A fabric, cut 2½in bias strips across the fabric, joined together on the bias to measure 325in (cut one end of the strip at a 45-degree angle), then fold it in half lengthwise (wrong sides together) and press it, making sure the raw fabric edges are aligned and parallel to create a French-fold for the binding.

23 Open out the end you have cut at 45 degrees, then turn under a ¼in hem, press the hem to the wrong side of the fabric and re-press the fold in the binding. This will be the end at which you start attaching the binding to the quilt.

24 Make sure the quilt is trimmed and squared after the quilting is complete.

25 For binding this quilt, we have used a ½in seam allowance. Measure ½in in from each side of each corner of the quilt and place a pin in the quilt on the vertical to mark the spot.

26 Start in the center of one side of the right side of the quilt, and place the right side of the binding over the quilt (starting with the hemmed edge of the binding) with the raw fabric edges of the binding and the quilt aligned and parallel. Pin the first two inches of the binding to the quilt. Next, with a ½in seam allowance, construction thread and foot, start attaching the binding to the quilt beyond the pins (this section will be attached to the quilt once the binding is joined at the end).

27 Sew the binding to the quilt until you reach the ½in pin mark from the first corner, then sew off the fabric at a 45-degree angle to the corner and remove the pin. Remove the quilt from the machine and fold the binding upwards and away from the quilt (the binding will fold back against the row of stitching that is at 45-degrees; see diagram below).

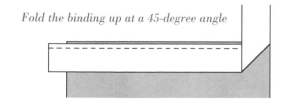

Fold the binding up at a 45-degree angle

28 Vertically pin-fold the binding (the head of the pin should be to the outside edge of the quilt and aligned with the cut edge of the quilt and binding), then bring the binding in line with the next side edge of the quilt (see diagram below).

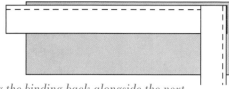

Bring the binding back alongside the next edge, creating a fold at the corner

29 Bring the quilt back to the machine and start sewing at the top edge of the quilt, then remove the pins. Continue around the quilt. When the binding reaches 2in from the starting point (of the binding, not the stitching), overlap the end of the binding over the beginning of the binding, making sure that it covers (on both sides of the binding and by 1in) the 45-degree angle edge that has been turned under, then cut the end of the binding at the same angle as the beginning of the binding.

30 Remove the pins from the beginning of the binding and open it out flat. Place the opened-out end of the binding over the inside of the beginning of the binding (right side of end of binding to wrong side of beginning of binding) so the raw fabric edges and the fold lines are aligned. Refold the binding, making sure it is flat. The length of the binding that needs to be sewn to the quilt now measures 4in (or the same as that of the quilt left to bind). Pin, making sure the raw fabric edges of the end of the binding are concealed under the hemmed edge of the beginning of the binding.

31 Use a hand-sewing needle to slip-stitch the hemmed edge of the binding overlap.

32 Press and then pin the binding to the back of the quilt. The corners of the binding will automatically form a mitered corner from both the back and front of the quilt. Use a hand-sewing needle to slip-stitch the binding to the back of the quilt, sewing the back mitered corners in place as you go.

33 Sign and date your quilt.

Congratulations – your voyage is at an end. You can now explore the vast land of machine-embroidered quilts. Who knows where your next voyage of creative discovery will take you and what magic waters you will sail. Wherever your voyage takes you, we know you are now an experienced sailor on the seas of creativity and will always take a little of Simon's Aquamarine Ambience with you.

Aquamarine Ambience

From the Captain's Table

Aquamarine Ambience table runner
Robyn Wilson and Jenny Haskins

This table runner is a fabulous way to use up the
circles that were cut from the frame fabric when you
made the Aquamarine Ambience quilt, and to learn
the Jenny Join – a great way to quilt-as-you-go.
It's also wonderful to work with your BSR
(Bernina Stitch Regulator) foot, and to experiment
with different quilting patterns.

Finished size of table runner: 12in x 36in

Materials

- Bernina Artista 730E embroidery machine and 255mm x 145mm hoop
- Bernina Artista Software V4 and transfer device
- Bernina gold-latch bobbin case to be used for embroidery
- *Aquamarine Ambience* design CD by Jenny Haskins (included with this book)
- 3, 15in squares of light green/blue nap silk dupione for frames (Color A)
- 3, 10in circles of dark green/blue nap silk dupione for insert circles (Color B) (the circles are left over from the *Aquamarine Ambience* quilt, having been cut from the center of the frame fabric)
- 3yd x 2½in bias binding in either dark or light blue–green fabric (this could also be left over from the *Aquamarine Ambience* quilt)
- 12in x 45in dark blue cotton backing fabric
- 1yd x 36in lightweight fusible batting
- Machine needle: Jeans 80
- Machine feet: darning foot No 26, patchwork ¼in foot No 37, open-toe appliqué foot No 20 and BSR (Bernina Stitch Regulator) foot No 42
- Threads: Robison-Anton rayon 40 embroidery threads: Bluestone (No 2515), Jungle Green (No 2597), Peapod (No 2456) and Green Forest (No 2451)
- Threads to match fabrics for construction, quilting and bobbins
- Pre-wound fine bobbins for embroidery, to reduce the bulk
- Self-adhesive tear-away stabilizer (must tear away easily and not be too sticky)
- Crisp tear-away stabilizer to back the decorative stitching around the circles
- *Cut A Round* tool (19in–6in) by Phillips Fiber Art
- *Sewing Revolution* (to round the ends of the table runner)
- 1 Clover chalk pencil in pink
- Rotary cutter (45mm), self-healing cutting mat and quilter's ruler
- Long fine glass-headed quilting pins
- Small thread clips
- Paper scissors to cut stabilizer
- Heavy-duty spray starch
- Vellum tracing paper to print placement templates
- Awl to punch holes in the placement templates
- Helmar's *Dust A Way* compressed air (to keep tension areas on the machine lint-free)
- Helmar's quilt basting spray to apply backing fabric to blocks
- Sticky tape
- Hand-sewing needle
- Blue and blue-green heat-activated crystals and heating wand to crystalise the center flowers in each block
- General sewing requirements

Preparation

1 Go to the Bernina website (**www.berninausa.com**). Select *What's New*, then *FREE Downloads*, then *Free Embroidery Hoop Basting Designs*, then the appropriate hoop size to suit your machine. Now download this to your computer (*Aquamarine Ambience* designs use the 255mm x 145mm oval hoop). Follow the directions found on the website on how to use the basting stitch in conjunction with your embroidery designs.

2 Use the Artista design software and transfer device to transfer designs aa16, aa08, aa09 and aa10 to the computer; add basting stitch to each design and then transfer the designs to the machine and print templates for each design.

JENNY'S TIP: Make sure you read and understand all the tips and technical information given in the Aquamarine Ambience *quilt instructions before going any further in this project.*

3 Go to pages 12-18 (in the instructions for the *Aquamarine Ambience* quilt) and read the directions for the following – Preparation, Embroidery, using the *Cut A Round* tool, vellum templates, tear-away self-adhesive (sticky) stabilizer, and *Jenny's Tricks of the Trade*. All materials used are listed in this project's materials list.

4 Use the rotary cutter, self-healing cutting mat and quilter's ruler to cut from the:

Color A fabric:

☼ three, 15in squares (for the frames)

☼ 2½in strips across the bias of the fabric and joined on the bias to measure 3yd (for the binding).

Color B fabric:

☼ three, 10in circles to insert into the frames.

Backing fabric:

☼ three, 15in squares to back the 15in squares with inserted circles.

5 Use the *Cut A Round* tool to cut a 9in circle in the center of each of the three 15in squares from the Color A fabric (for the frames), then insert the three 10in circles from the Color B fabric into the frames, referring to pages 12-15 for directions on cutting and inserting circles into frames.

6 Iron the 15in squares of fusible batting to the back of the 15in squares with inserted circles.

Stitch-building

7 Each 15in square (frame with inserted circle) backed with fusible batting has decorative stitching sewn over the top of the seam, around the inserted circle.

8 Use the open-toe appliqué foot No 20, a pre-wound bobbin in the gold-latch bobbin case, the Jeans 80 needle threaded with rayon 40 embroidery thread, and crisp tear-away stabilizer at the back of the circles for all decorative stitching.

JENNY'S TIP: When sewing around a curve (especially using decorative stitching), the shorter the length of the pattern or stitch the easier it is to get an accurate curve. Remember to pivot with the needle in the down position for tight curves, at the end of each stitch pattern. A pattern length of below 10mm is the easiest to handle; 6mm is the optimum pattern length.

9 Label the blocks 1 to 3 from left to right (refer to the flat picture of the table runner), and mark the top of each block to ensure the nap of the fabric is consistent for circles and frames.

10 Sew decorative stitching around each circle in all three blocks:

Block 1

☼ stitch 407 (oval-shaped satin stitch), width 4.6, length 0.1, pattern extend 2, using Jungle Green (No 2597)

☼ stitch 623 (overlapping arrow heads), width 2, length 1.4, centred over the top of stitch 407, using Peapod (No 2456)

Block 2

☼ stitch 405 (step-satin-stitch squares), width 6, length 0.1, pattern extend 2, using Peapod (No 2456)

☼ stitch 711 (lazy daisy stitch), width 3, length 1.7, centred over the top of stitch 405, using Jungle Green (No 2597)

Block 3

☼ memory stitch 401, width 6, length 0.3, flipped vertically; and stitch 401, width 6, length 0.3, using (satin-stitch diamond) Jungle Green (No 2597)

☼ stitch 353 (hem stitch), width 1.5, length 1, centred over the top of the memory stitch 401, using Peapod (No 2456)

11 Remove all tear-away stabilizer from the back of the decorative stitching and press each block.

Embroidery

12 Use the self-adhesive tear-away stabilizer in the hoop, a pre-wound bobbin in the gold-latch bobbin case, rayon 40 embroidery thread in the Jeans 80 needle and the darning foot No 26 for all embroidery.

13 Make sure you have the basting stitch around your two embroidery designs before transferring them to the sewing machine.

Block 1

14 Center the vellum template for design aa16 over the center of the block, making sure the leaves are centred on each side of all divide lines marked on the fabric.

15 Place the hoop in the machine, center the needle over the design, and place the fabric over the stabilizer (matching vertical and horizontal lines on the fabric with those marked on the hoop). Stitch the basting stitch first, then the embroidery design in the following sequence:

☼ color 1 leaves – Peapod (No 2456)

☼ color 2 flower – Jungle Green (No 2597)

☼ color 3 center of flower – Peapod (No 2456)

Press the block and put it to one side.

Block 2

16 Combine templates for designs aa08 and aa09. Design aa08 sits horizontally across the vertical design aa09 to form one circular design (refer to the photo as a guide). Hold the templates together with sticky tape. Center the combined templates over the center of block 2 and mark the positions for both embroidery designs.

17 Embroider design aa08 first, with the basting stitch sewn first and the colors next in the following sequence:

☼ color 1 large leaves – Peapod (No 2456)

☼ color 2 small leaves – Jungle Green (No 2597).

18 Remove the hoop from the machine and the fabric from the hoop and then press the block. Replace the combination template over the center of the block, placing the template for design aa08 over the actual embroidered design aa08 to check its placement before embroidering the next design. If the position for the next

design has changed, re-mark the placement lines for the next embroidery.

19 Embroider design aa09 second, with the basting stitch sewn first and the colors next in the following sequence:

☼ color 1 large leaves – Peapod (No 2456)

☼ color 2 small leaves – Jungle Green (No 2597)

☼ color 3 cactus shapes – Green Forest (No 2451)

☼ color 4 tiny outside leaves – Green Forest (No 2451)

☼ color 5 small flowers – Peapod (No 2456)

☼ color 6 tiny center leaves – Peapod (No 2456)

☼ color 7 center flower – Bluestone (No 2515)

Press the block and put it to one side.

Block 3

20 Center the vellum template for design aa10 over the center of the block, making sure a flower is centred on each divide line marked on the fabric.

21 Place the hoop in the machine, center the needle over the design, and place the fabric over the stabilizer (matching vertical and horizontal lines on the fabric with those marked on the hoop). Stitch the basting stitch first, then the colors next in the following sequence:

☼ color 1 outside leaves – Peapod (No 2456)

☼ color 2 outside flower – Jungle Green (No 2597)

☼ color 3 inner leaves – Green Forest (No 2451)

☼ color 4 inner flowers – Peapod (No 2456)

☼ color 5 circle – Jungle Green (No 2597)

☼ color 6 center leaf – Peapod (No 2456)

☼ color 7 center flower – Green Forest (No 2451)

Press the block and put it to one side.

Quilting

22 Use Helmar's quilt basting spray to apply the 15in squares of backing fabric to each of the three embroidered blocks.

23 Use the BSR foot No 42, Jeans 80 needle threaded with Jungle Green (No 2597), thread in the bobbin to match the backing fabric in the gold-latch bobbin case, and a straight stitch to freehand-quilt the blocks.

24 Blocks 1 to 3: the frame fabric only (up to the circular fabric) on each block is quilted with a continuous swirling design.

Blocks 1 and 3 are quilted to look like bubbles by using a continuous circle design on the outside edge of the embroidery design (on the circle fabric only).

25 When the quilting is complete, press each block and square it up to 12in.

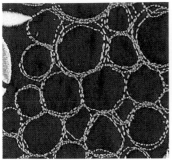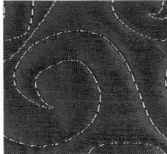

The Jenny Join

26 The *Jenny Join* is easy; it allows you to quilt-as-you-go, it gives you flat seams with no bulk, and it is both decorative and functional.

☀ Lay blocks 1 and 2 together (making sure both blocks are up the correct way) so the edges to be joined are butted up together and the pieces to be joined are aligned on each end.

☀ Use quilting pins to hold the two pieces together – put them through one quilt piece and then pass them through the seam line into the other quilt piece. Pins are placed horizontally to the seam.

> *JENNY'S TIP: It is important to center and keep all stitch rows straight at all times when using this technique. Stitch-building requires that all rows of stitching are straight, aligned and parallel to each other or centred over the previous row of stitching. The effect is that of one row of stitching to form a braid, lace or ribbon.*

27 Use the open-toe appliqué foot No 20, the Jeans 80 needle, and thread that matches the thread in the gold-latch bobbin case to sew from the front of the table runner in the following sequence:

☀ stitch 11, width 2.5, length 1.5, in Peapod (No 2456), centred over the two raw fabric edges of the blocks that are butted up together

☀ stitch 11, width 8, length 0.6, in Peapod (No 2456), centred over the seam

☀ stitch 308, width 8, length 3.5, in Jungle Green (No 2597), centred over the 9mm satin stitch 11

☀ stitch 11, width 2, length 0.6, in Peapod (No 2456), on each side of the 9mm stitch 11

☀ stitch 407, width 3, length 0.1, in Jungle Green (No 2597), on each side of the 2mm stitch 11

28 Join block 3 to block 2 in the same way. Press the table runner.

Finishing the table runner

29 Use a Sewing Revolution and rotary cutter to slightly round each corner on both ends of the table runner.

30 Bind the quilt with a French binding using the 3yd x 2½in bias strip, folded in half and then stitched around the edge of the table runner with the right sides of the binding and the right side of the runner together; raw fabric edges of both must be aligned and sewn from the wrong side of the binding using construction thread in the needle and bobbin and the patchwork ¼in foot No 37.

31 Turn the binding to the back of the runner and use the hand-sewing needle to slip-stitch it in place.

32 You may choose to sew decorative stitching, as we have, around the edge of the table runner on the seam line of the binding, remembering to match the bobbin thread to the needle thread and using the open-toe appliqué foot No 20 in the following sequence:

☀ stitch 424, alternating blocks stitch, width 6, length 1, using Peapod (No 2456) centred over the binding seam line

☀ stitch 623 (overlapping arrow heads), width 2, length 1.4, centred over the top of stitch 424, using Jungle Green (No 2597).

> *We trust you have enjoyed the techniques learned in this project, especially using the BSR for quilting and the Jenny Join to join your blocks – what amazing possibilities these two wonders have for us mere mortals to shine like the stars!*

BSR

The **Bernina Stitch Regulator (BSR)** *is a revolutionary foot that attaches to a domestic sewing/embroidery machine, world patented and exclusive to Bernina, designed to fit model numbers: 440, 630, 640, 200 and 730 sewing machines. This amazing attachment allows a freehand machine-quilter to master in minutes what used to require hours of practice – that is consistent free-motion stitching.*

The BSR attachment takes the fear factor out of free-motion machine-quilting, as it automatically regulates the stitch length (all stitches have the same length) adjusting the stitch length in direct ratio to the speed at which the quilter moves the fabric under the needle. This results in free-motion stitching/quilting that has uniform stitch lengths.

Working well with all types and sizes of fabric the BSR comes with variable speed, adjustable stitch length and width (on machine models with zigzag BSR) as well as the option of 'cruise control' there is no need to use a foot control; instead, the use the start/stop button on the machine gives the quilting artist the control and freedom to concentrate on exploring creativity. All one has to do is move the fabric rather than the machine, so the focus is on the project.

Using cutting-edge technology with the fine tradition of Bernina quality, the BSR is a foot that attaches to the machine, is light, compact and user friendly as well as easy to learn and operate. The fabric is moved under the needle rather than the machine over the fabric, which maximizes space at hand and eliminates the need to house a free-standing frame (although it works well with the Aurora range of machines and frames).

The Bernina Stitch Regulator is a must for any quilter who wants to master free-motion stitching and quilting so why wait when the BSR is knocking at your sewing studio door – all you have to do is open the door to total BSR free-motion freedom!

From the Captain's Bunk

Port Wine Pillow
Robyn Wilson and Jenny Haskins

*By now we all know
that any shade of purple is Jenny's
favorite color, and port wine
is no exception.
This little pillow is yet another color
combination that can be used
with the techniques you learned in
Aquamarine Ambience.
The thread shades combined with silk
and velvet in similar and contrasting
colors result in a feast of texture,
embroidery and quilting.*

*All the materials needed
to make this pillow, and the techniques
used, are covered in the* Aquamarine
Ambience *quilt, pillow and table runner,
so only the fabric measurements,
thread colors and embroidery and
quilting designs used will be given to
make this delightful little pillow.*

Materials

- 12in square of nap silk: purple napped with black frame fabric
- 12in square of nap silk: lavender napped with dark purple circle fabric
- 2, 2½in strips of patterned velvet across the width of the fabric for the pillow borders
- 12in square of fusible batting
- 8in diameter circle of fusible batting
- 30in x 15in strip of backing fabric
- 12in pillow insert
- ⅔yd heather-coloured ½in-wide circular trim to embellish around the center embroidery design in the pillow top
- Embroidery designs aa40 and aa22 from the *Aquamarine Ambience* design CD by Jenny Haskins (included with this book)
- Threads: Robison-Anton rayon 40 threads: Intense Maroon (No 2587), Metallic Gold (No 1003), Ducky Mauve (No 2422) and Heather (No 2271)
- Vellum tracing paper to print a template of design aa22, which is used to mark the corner placement position for this design.

Preparation

1   Cut a 7in circle in the 12in purple nap silk for the frame fabric and an 8in circle from the lavender silk for the circle insert, then stitch the circle to the frame fabric.

2   Fuse the 8in circle of batting to the back of the 8in lavender nap silk circle, then fuse the 12in batting square to the back of the 12in purple nap silk square.

3   From the 2½in strips of patterned velvet, cut the following for the borders of the pillow:

☼   two, 11in strips for the top and bottom of the pillow

☼   two, 15in strips for the sides of the pillow.

4   Print the template for design aa22.

Decorative stitching

5   Use Ducky Mauve (No 2422) to sew a satin-stitch ball stitch (width and length 6), centred over the seam line of the 8in circle.

Quilting

6   Use the darning foot No 26 and Ducky Mauve (No 2422) to quilt the lavender circle in the center of the pillow top, using a swirling MacTavishing quilting design.

Embroidery

7   Embroider design aa40 in the center of the lavender circle in the following color sequence:

☼   color 1 center flower – Intense Maroon (No 2587)

☼   color 2 center of flower – Metallic Gold (No 1003)

Remove the fabric from the hoop, press it, and then re-hoop the stabiliser to embroider the next design.

8   Use the placement template for design aa22 to mark the embroidery position for this design centred in each corner of the pillow top on the diagonal lines. Use the photo as guide and note that the point of the center large leaf just touches the decorative stitching around the quilted circle insert in the pillow top.

9   Embroider design aa40 centred in each corner of the pillow top, using a fresh piece of stabiliser in the hoop for each new design, in the following color sequence:

- color 1 large center leaf – Intense Maroon (No 2587)
- color 2 flower at bottom of leaf – Gold Metallic (No 1003)
- color 3 small side leaves – Ducky Mauve (No 2422)
- color 4 small side flowers – Heather (No 2271)

Embroider all four designs in this fashion, removing excess stabiliser from the back of each embroidery and pressing the fabric before moving on to the next corner.

10 Square up the pillow top to 11in.

11 Attach the ⅔yd of ½in circular heather braid in a circle around the center embroidery using the photo as a guide.

Construction

12 Use the patchwork ¼in foot to join the pattern velvet borders to the 11in square embroidered pillow top:

- 11in x 2½in strip to the top and bottom of the square
- 15in x 2½in strip to the sides of the square.

13 Press the seam to the outside edge of the pillow.

14 Fold under a ½in double hem on each 15in end of the 25in strip of pillow backing fabric, then cut this into two 11½in x 15in rectangles. Overlap these two fabric pieces (wrong side of top fabric piece to right side of bottom fabric piece), to form a 15in square. Pin them, then stitch down the overlap on each side of the 15in pillow backing.

15 Attach the pillow back to the pillow top, right sides together and stitching around the four sides, then turn the pillow to the right side and press it.

16 Stitch-in-the-ditch through all layers of fabric in the border seam lines, then top-stitch around

the outside edge of the pillow, ¼in in from the edge of the velvet borders.

17 Place the insert into the pillow.

Port Wine Pillow is perfect for that special chair in your boudoir – the place you find peace and tranquility at the end of the day, and where you can reflect on Aquamarine Ambience and plunge into its depth of color and design.

From the Captain's Galley

Pink Grapefruit with a Twist of Lime
Jenny Haskins and Robyn Wilson

How can anyone resist color?
It is a temptress to the eye, exciting the soul
and stimulating creativity in the heart
of any true artist.
The two nap silk fabrics used in the
Pink Grapefruit with a Twist of Lime
pillow are truly 'candy for the eyes',
and a must to be teamed together
along with threads in colors that complement
the embroidery and enhance the quilting.

All the materials needed to make this pillow, and the techniques used, are covered in the Aquamarine Ambience quilt, pillow and table runner, so only the fabric measurements, thread colors and embroidery and quilting designs used will be given to make this delightful little pillow.

Materials

- ⊚ 12in square of nap silk: apricot napped with lime green frame fabric
- ⊚ 12in square of nap silk: lime green napped with hot pink circle fabric
- ⊚ 6in strips across the width of the lime green napped with hot pink silk, joined to measure 2⅓yd (for the double frill)
- ⊚ 12in square of fusible batting
- ⊚ 8in diameter circle of fusible batting
- ⊚ 24in x 12in strip of backing fabric
- ⊚ 10in pillow insert
- ⊚ Embroidery design aa26 from the *Aquamarine Ambience* design CD by Jenny Haskins (included with this book)
- ⊚ Threads: Robison-Anton rayon 40 embroidery threads: Pro Cinnamon (No 2611), TH Burgundy (No 2608), Salmon (No 2299) and Tamarack (No 2230)

Preparation

1 Cut a 7in circle in the apricot nap silk for the frame fabric and an 8in circle from the lime nap silk for the circle insert, then stitch the circle to the frame fabric.

2 Fuse the 8in circle of batting to the back of the 8in lime nap silk circle.

Decorative stitching

3 Use Tamarack (No 2230) thread to sew a satin stitch scallop around the seam line of the 8in circle so the scallops face to the edge of the pillow and the straight edge of the scallop is aligned with and follows the circle seam line.

Embroidery

4 Embroider design aa26 in the center of the lime circle in the following color sequence:

- ☀ color 1 center flower – Pro Cinnamon (No 2611)
- ☀ color 2 center of flower – TH Burgundy (No 2608)
- ☀ color 3 large leaves – Salmon (No 2299)
- ☀ color 4 small leaves – Tamarack (No 2230)
- ☀ color 5 small flowers – TH Burgundy (No 2608)

Quilting

5   Fuse the 12in square of fusible batting to the back of the embroidered square, then use the BSR foot and Pro Cinnamon (No 2611) to freehand-quilt the frame fabric using the swirling MacTavishing quilting design.

6   Press the pillow and then square up the top to 10½in.

Construction

7   Join the 2⅛yd x 6in lime frill fabric into a circle and then fold it in half width-wise. Press it, then gather it up to 4ft and stitch it to the outside edge of the pillow (aligning the raw fabric edges on the right side of the frill with those on the right side of the pillow top, and stitching from the wrong side of the frill).

8   Make up the pillow backing using the overlapping technique from the *Finding Your Sea Legs* pillow, and attach the backing to the pillow right sides of backing fabric and pillow top together, and stitching around all four sides.

9   Turn the pillow cover to the right side, press it and place the pillow insert inside.

The Pink Grapefruit with a Twist of Lime *pillow is a perfect porch pillow!
There you are – it's a sunny afternoon,
you're sipping on pink grapefruit juice
with a twist of fresh lime and overlooking
the sparking waters of Aquamarine
Ambience – bliss!*

A 12-Gun Salute to...

Nothing just happens on its own - there is always a cast of (what often seems like) thousands behind any venture, and Jenny and Simon would like to salute and thank the talented team that supports them and have helped make this book happen almost overnight.

Editor: Jenny Haskins
Quilt by: Simon Haskins

Publisher: Thanks to Simon Blackall and Diane Wallis, the talented duo from The Watermark Press who always know what to do when it comes to publishing, and then do it with class. Thank you for being part of *Aquamarine Ambience.*

Designer: Suzy King of Suzy King Design is the magic designer behind all Jenny's and Simon's books and magazines. Her special flair and ability to get inside Jenny's head and improve on it is a rare gift indeed - perhaps she could market this!

Subeditor: Nina Paine is able to take what is written and edit it in such a way that it is clear and to the point, yet retains Jenny's warm and fuzzy 'voice', making it a pleasure to read. (It also makes the author look really good!)

Photographer: Tom Evangelidis, photographer extraordinaire! Tom captures the mood, color and style in every shot, thus making anything he photographs look better than the real thing. Keep him warm and well-fed and Tom can turn out magic photography with classic charm and style that reflects his Greek ancestry.

Photographer: Laurie Haskins (Simon's dad) is not only a great father but a wonderful photographer as well. Laurie takes pride in taking wonderful seascape photographs, spending hours to get the light just right both in the sky and on the water, making each picture perfect. It seemed only fitting then to feature some of Laurie's

Australian seascapes in his son's book. Thank you also Laurie for allowing Tom to photograph the fantastic tall ships from your collection – they certainly add charm and atmosphere to *Aquamarine Ambience.*

Stylist: Robyn Wilson (with a little help from Jenny). What do we say about you Robbie – your warmth, friendship and creative talent endear you to all who cross your path, and your talent as a stylist is reflected in every picture Tom takes. Added to this, you are part of this book in another way, making projects, keeping Jenny calm and just being you – thank you for keeping us all on track and being so very special.

Marge Boyle of Quilters' Resource, a friend and colleague of Jenny's and Simon's for over 10 years. Marge has a special place (both personally and professionally) in Jenny's and Simon's hearts and they would like to thank her for her loyalty and support over the years.

Kevin Anderson and Kerrie Hay of Bernina Australia are two of the most generous, giving and supporting people in the sewing industry in

Australia, as well as being friends and colleagues. Nothing is ever too much trouble and Jenny and Simon could not have done this book without their support and friendship.

Gayle Hillert of Bernina USA, whose gentle ways and giving spirit touch all who come in contact with her; this book is a tribute to Gayle's strength and generosity.

Andreea Sparhawk of Robison-Anton threads, who is responsible for Jenny and Simon using glorious RA threads in this book and all their projects. The success of any project is dependant on color and design, and RA lights up the life of any project with shimmering colors that reflect the personality of the artist and confirm the quality and range of RA threads to all who use them.

You are now a seasoned sailor!
Set sail on a new quilting voyage,
so keep your eyes peeled for
Jenny and Simon's
next exciting and enticing quilt!

The Jenny Haskins
Design Collection
Showing the way to your creative journey

 bella fiori

 beyond color purple

 color purple the next generation

 designer neck ties & other continuous designs

 floral appliqué magic — With more than 250 designs!!

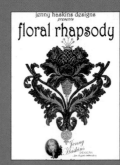 floral rhapsody

 lace glorious lace

 rose buds

 roses for mary

 twin needle shadow work by machine

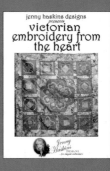 victorian bows & baskets

victorian embroidery from the heart

 victorian fantasy with fans

 victorian pansies

 victorian piano shawl

 Jenny Haskins DESIGNS ...for elegant embroidery

 victorian roses

 victorian script & antique frames

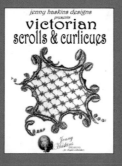 victorian scrolls & curlicues

Available from:

Unique Creative Opportunities (Aust)

Phone +621 9680 1381
Fax +621 9680 1381
Email jenny@rpi.net.au
www.jennyhaskins.com

Quilters' Resource (US)

Phone 1800 676 6543
www.quiltersresource.com

 antique cutwork lace

 art nouveau series: iris

 art nouveau series: spring flowers

Books by
Jenny Haskins

Victorian Dreams
Sally Milner Publications

Color Purple (out of print) see Creative
Expressions No 12 & No 13 for directions

Amadeus Aussie Publishing

Inspirational Machine Embroidered Quilting
(Arsenic and Old Lace Quilt) Aussie Publishing

Victorian Pansies Quilters' Resource

Victorian Roses Quilters' Resource

Victorian Splendor Quilters' Resource

Inspirational Home Décor Brother Australia

Latté Quilt with Kerrie Hay Quilters' Resource

Roses for Mary Quilters' Resource

MarJen for Error Pride Publishing

Simon's Folly Pride Publishing

Aquamarine Ambience
Quilters' Resource